THE STEP BY STEP ART OF
Papier Mâché

CLB 3108
This edition published in 1994 by Coombe Books
©1993 CLB Publishing Ltd, Godalming, Surrey
Printed and bound in Singapore
All rights reserved
ISBN 1-85833-104-8

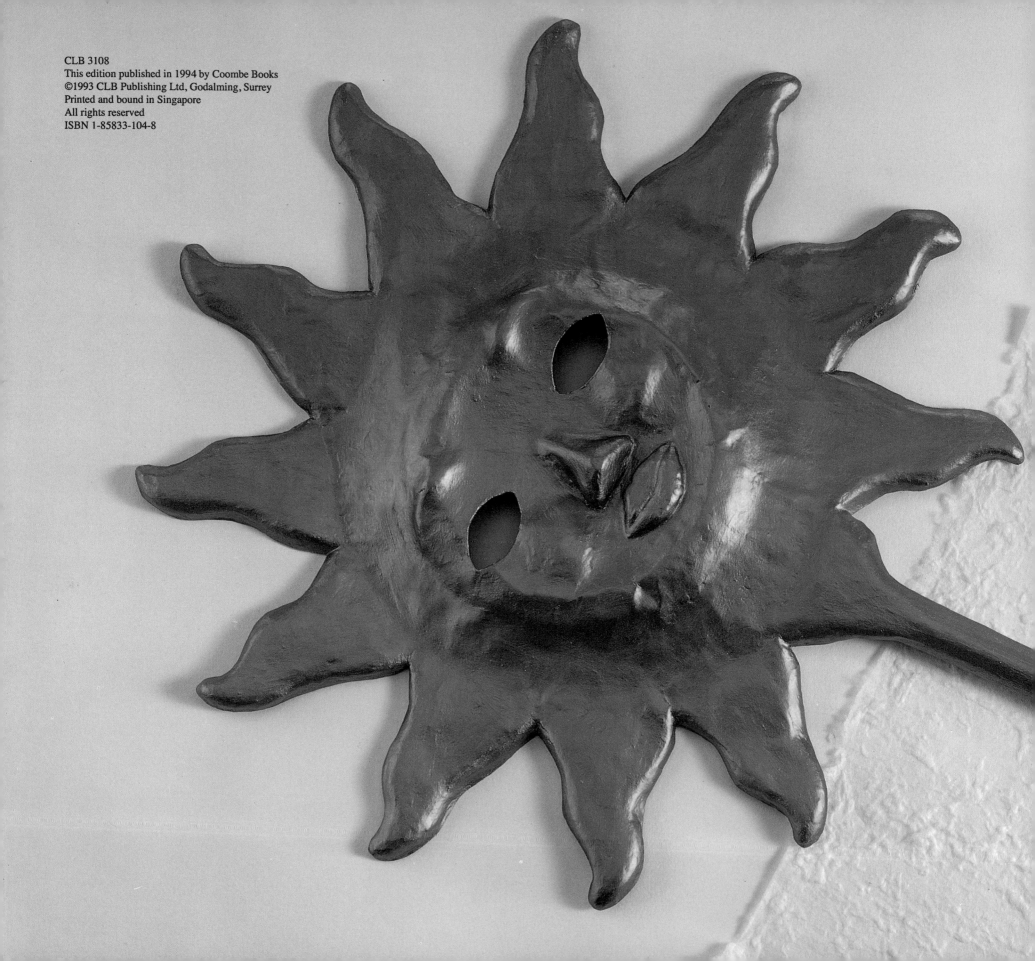

THE STEP BY STEP ART OF
Papier Mâché

Text and Papier Mâché Designs by
CHERYL OWEN

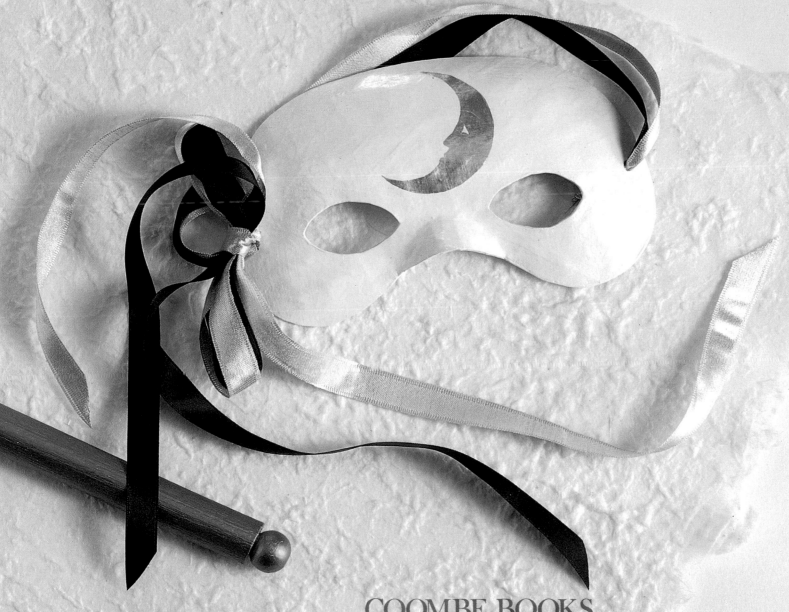

COOMBE BOOKS

Contents

Introduction

Papier mâché is an enormously versatile and exciting craft medium. Much of its appeal is based on the simplicity of the techniques used and the ready availability of the materials needed – newspaper is the main ingredient. The projects in this book are constructed using two basic methods: layered papier mâché where strips of newspaper are built up in layers, and papier mâché pulp where torn pieces of newspaper are soaked in water and pulped. Papier mâché pulp can be modelled rather like clay.

All the projects are accompanied by easy-to-follow step-by-step instructions and drawings, with the main techniques used throughout the book covered in a separate section.

Materials

Paper and Card

Collect together a supply of old newspapers. Generally, broadsheet papers are made of a higher quality paper and are more suited to making papier mâché than tabloid papers.

Use **tracing paper** to trace any templates needed from the back of the book. Transfer the design using the tracing paper if the transferred outline is likely to be visible. Transfer the design using carbon paper if it will not show.

Various thicknesses of card are needed to make moulds. **Corrugated card** from old boxes is very durable and can be obtained free from stores and supermarkets. **Mounting**

board is smooth to the touch and of a much finer quality than corrugated card. It is available in different thicknesses and can be purchased from art suppliers. If thick card is required, it should be sturdy enough to crease if bent. Since thick card does not fold easily, you will need to score along the line of the fold with a craft knife first to ensure a straight crease.

If you need to create a template, use thin, **lightweight card** such as that used for cereal packets.

Save any left-over **giftwrap** or **printed paper bags** since these are useful for applying a final layer of papier mâché. **Tissue paper** is rather delicate but an interesting effect can be achieved when layers are overlapped. Colourful **gummed paper** is used in many of the projects in this book.

Sophisticated projects often benefit from the use of unusual paper. Specialist art suppliers stock a range of **textured paper**, which, although more expensive, add an extra dimension to a hand-crafted model.

Paints

Most of the projects in this book are painted. **Craft paints** are versatile and come in a range of glossy, pearlized, metallic or matt finishes. The colours mix easily, dry quickly and most are non-toxic.

Acrylic paints and **spray paints** are also very effective. Always spray in a well-ventilated room and protect the surrounding area with newspaper. Please use sprays that are free from CFCs.

Indian inks give a translucent effect and colours can be easily blended together. **Relief paints** (see page 21) are available in tubes or bottles and are great fun to experiment with.

Craft Accessories

Most craft and jewellery components are inexpensive and can be found in craft and haberdashery stores.

Toy making accessories, such as eyes, noses and whiskers, are highly realistic and are useful in making papier-mâché animals. **Stamen strings** are short strings with solid, coloured ends used in the making of artificial flowers.

Look out for interesting decorations. **Beads, jewellery stones** and **sequins** all give a theatrical feel. **Sequin dust** – the tiny circles left after sequins have been pressed out – can be used for added sparkle.

Equipment

Much of the equipment needed for papier mâché falls within the standard desk range, which you probably already possess. For comfort and safety, work on a flat, clean surface, keeping sharp implements, glues and paints well out of reach of children.

For Drawing and Cutting

A **propelling pencil** or sharpened **HB pencil** is best for drawing. Always use a **ruler** and **set square** when drawing squares and rectangles so that any angles are accurate. Draw circles with a **compass** or use a **circle stencil** for miniature circles.

Sharp, **pointed scissors** are very useful. A **craft knife** will give a neater cut but remember always to use it on a cutting mat or sheet of corrugated card. Replace the blade often – a blunt blade will tear the paper or card. Retain blunt blades since they are useful for cutting plastic clay.

For Sticking

Brown paper tape is used to join pieces of card. **Masking tape** is a low-tack tape. It can be used to hold paper and templates in position and later removed without marking the surface of your work.

PVA medium (polyvinyl acetate), available at art and craft stores, is a non-toxic adhesive that dries to a clear, glossy finish. In papier mâché, a solution of PVA medium thinned with water is used for sticking down the paper strips. PVA medium in concentrated form is used for sticking down papier mâché pulp and as a varnish and sealant.

The layered papier-mâché projects in this book all use PVA solution but wallpaper paste or flour and water are acceptable alternatives.

Papier mâché made with PVA medium can be hardened quickly in a microwave oven if it has been modelled over a card mould. Never heat the model in the oven for longer than one minute at a time and do not leave the oven unattended.

PVA medium can be brushed onto newspaper strips which can then be used as a tape to join card pieces together.

Always store PVA medium in an airtight container when not in use.

Use an all-purpose **household glue** to attach jewellery stones, braid and other accessories. **Extra strong adhesive** is useful for sticking pieces that need a stronger bond.

For Modelling

Plastic clay is used for modelling moulds. Other moulds are constructed from card or can incorporate **polystyrene** ball, cone and egg shapes or lightweight **cotton pulp balls**. Objects such as bowls, plates, balloons and pipe cleaners can also be used as moulds.

Some moulds will need to be removed with the help of a coating of **petroleum jelly**.

A blunt **craft knife blade** is useful for modelling as are **manicure implements**. Much of the modelling will be done by hand.

Wood dowelling is available in different thicknesses. Cover with papier mâché or paint.

Chicken wire can be moulded into various shapes. Use wire cutters to cut the wire.

To Finish

The completed model can be sanded down for a smooth finish with sandpaper or, for intricate areas, a nail file. Use **wood filler** to even out the papier-mâché surface if you prefer a level finish.

Use household **emulsion paint** or **gesso** for undercoating. Gesso, available from art stores, is more expensive but dries quickly and gives a thicker layer of paint.

A range of paintbrushes will be needed for different purposes. An old brush can be used for PVA solution when applying layered papier mâché. Good quality artist's brushes for painting are worth the expense – use a fine brush for details.

Brass paper fasteners, available from stationers, are a simple way of fastening card and can also be used as decoration. **Screw-eyes**, from hardware stores, also have both practical and decorative applications.

Many of the finished projects will need to be varnished. Choose a varnish to suit the paper or paint finish. **Polyurethane varnish** is most versatile, although it does have a yellowing effect. It is available in gloss, satin or matt finishes.

Techniques

The same basic techniques occur in many of the projects. Before you start any project, carefully read the techniques described here and practise the methods needed. It is also helpful to begin by studying the photographs of the finished projects and by reading through the step-by-step instructions that appear with each project.

Cutting and Scoring

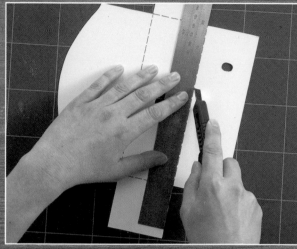

1 Work on a cutting mat or piece of corrugated card set on a flat, stable surface. If cutting with a **craft knife**, do not press too hard or attempt to cut right through thick card at the first approach but gradually cut deeper and deeper. If using a **scoring knife** do not cut right through the card but break the top surface only. Cut straight edges against a steel ruler.

Card Mould Method

1 Simple three-dimensional moulds can be made from card for the papier mâché models. Cut **brown paper tape** into short lengths. Moisten the tape.

2 Hold the pieces of card to be joined edge to edge. Stick the pieces of brown paper tape over the join, then smooth down with your finger.

Modelling Plastic Clay

1 Plastic clay is very useful for creating moulds for papier mâché projects. It is economical as it can be reused when the mould is finished with. Knead the clay to soften it before use. Mould the clay in your hands or use a rolling pin or milk bottle to roll the clay out flat.

2 An old knife or blunt craft knife is useful for cutting the clay. Hold a template on the rolled out clay and cut around the edges.

3 Round off the cut edges by patting them with a finger. Define any straight edges by patting with the side of a knife.

Using a Releasing Agent

1 *To remove papier mâché from a mould, the mould must first be covered with a releasing agent such as* **petroleum jelly.** *Use a cotton bud to apply the releasing agent into tight corners. Liquid detergent can be applied as an alternative to petroleum jelly.*

Layered Method

1 *Many types of paper can be used to make papier mâché but newspaper is the most versatile. Tear the paper into strips along the grain of the paper. A large flat surface such as the backgammon board (page 30) can be covered with strips 5 cm (2 in) wide but areas with corners or curves may need strips as narrow as 3 mm (⅛ in). It may be necessary to tear the strips into squares for some models.*

2 *To apply the first layer, thin some PVA medium with a little water in an old container. Brush the solution onto the strips and lay them in the same direction across the mould, overlapping the strips. Use a knife or cocktail stick to press the strips into tight corners. Leave to dry. When not in use, cover the PVA solution with baking (aluminum) foil to prevent it from drying out.*

3 *Brush the PVA solution onto the previous layer before applying further layers. If you can use a different coloured paper for alternate layers this will help differentiate between layers. Apply each layer at a different angle to the last to help strengthen the model. Strips can extend beyond the edges of a mould and can then be trimmed level with scissors or a craft knife when the papier mâché is dry.*

Pulp Method

1 Tear four double sheets of newspaper into pieces approximately 2.5 cm (1 in) square at the largest. Soak the pieces in water for at least eight hours, then boil in a saucepan for 20 minutes to loosen the fibres. Tip the solution into a sieve and shake out the excess water.

2 Use a whisk or blender to blend the paper pieces to a pulp. Empty the pulp into a mixing bowl. Add three tablespoons of PVA medium, one tablespoon of linseed oil and three drops of oil of cloves to help prevent mould forming.

3 Mix together with a spoon, squashing the pulp into a solid lump. Now squeeze the pulp together in your hands. Keep the pulp in an airtight container in the fridge when not in use. As an alternative to making your own pulp, paper pulp, available from art and craft stores or suppliers, can be mixed with water to produce a versatile, hard-wearing papier mâché pulp.

Cut and Rejoin Method

1 *If you have used a mould which needs to be removed from a covering of layered papier mâché, slice through the layers with a craft knife to separate the papier mâché into sections. You will end up with two sections from most moulds, but detailed models such as the elephants on page 44 are cut into three pieces. Where possible, cut through the flattest area of papier mâché as this will make rejoining easier.*

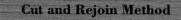

Sanding, Filling and Undercoating

1 *Using fine sandpaper, gently sand away any burrs and obvious unevenness on the model. A nail file is very useful for smaller models or corners.*

2 *If you want a smooth, level finish to the design, prepare some wood filler according to the manufacturer's instructions. Smear the filler onto the model and set aside to harden. Sand the model again.*

2 *Carefully pull the sections apart and remove the mould. Clay can be scooped out of fine detailing with a cotton bud.*

3 *Now rejoin the sections by holding them edge to edge and brush over the join with PVA solution. Completely reassemble the model by sticking short lengths of newspaper over the join. Further layers of papier mâché will need to be applied to reinforce the join.*

3 *A layer of undercoat will prepare the surface for painting. Household undercoat or gesso, available from art stores or suppliers, can be used for this. Apply a second and third coat if the model is to be painted with Indian inks or if it necessary to even out the surface a little more.*

Sponting

1 *The application of paint with a sponge is a very simple way of producing an interesting effect. Brush a thin film of paint onto an old plate or tile. Dab at the paint lightly with a damp natural sponge, taking care not to pick up too much paint or the result will be too dense.*

2 *Now dab the paint onto the model. If you are using a stencil, tape it in place with masking tape and dab with the sponge through the stencil cut-outs. Brush more paint onto the plate when necessary but do not apply it too thickly.*

Relief Paint

1 There are many exciting craft paints available today which can be used on paper and fabrics. Tubes and bottles of relief paint can be applied either using a brush or straight from the container's nozzle. The paint can be applied thickly so that it hardens raised from the papier mâché surface, or it can be applied with a fine paintbrush, stroking the paint outwards to give a soft, feathery effect. Experiment with different types of relief paints, including pearlized, crystal and glitter paints.

2 To add small decorations such as beads, sequins, jewellery stones or tiny shells, apply a spot of glitter or crystal relief paint and position the decoration with a pair of tweezers. When used on fabric, painted areas can be cut through without fear of the fabric fraying as the paint seals the fabric fibres.

21

Plant Life

The flowers and plants that provide artists with constant inspiration can be modelled from papier mâché in a stylized or realistic form. Papier mâché is also an ideal medium for the containers that hold our favourite dried or fresh flowers.

1 *To make the flower pot, cut off the lower section of a plastic carton or bottle. Following the layered method on page 16, apply five layers of papier mâché, sticking the ends of the newspaper strips to the inside of the pot and to the underside of the base. Leave to dry. Refer to the template on page 106 to cut a bow tie. Cut a strip of thin card 6.5 x 2 cm (2⅝ x ¾ in).*

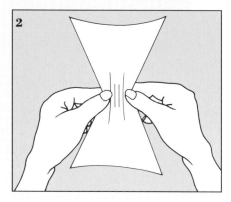

2 *To form the bow tie, fold along the broken lines bringing the folds to meet at the centre. Glue in place. Wrap the strip of card around the centre and glue the ends behind the bow tie. Apply four layers of papier mâché to the bow tie, trimming the edges level with the card when dry. Leave to dry then glue the bow tie to the pot. Undercoat and then paint the flower pot.*

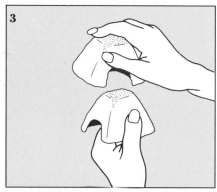

3 *For the hat, cut two sections from a cardboard egg carton to serve as the hat crown. Glue one section inside the other, swivelling the sections so there are no gaps. Cut a circle of thin card 11 cm (4½ in) in diameter.*

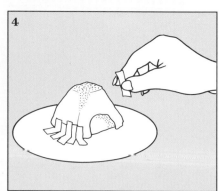

4 *Attach the crown to the centre of the circle using strips of newspaper and PVA medium. Bend two opposite sides of the circle upwards then cover the hat with four layers of papier mâché, following the layered method on page 16 and trimming excess papier mâché level with the edges of the brim. Pierce a hole in the centre of the hat, insert a garden stick into the hole and paint the hat. Cut a flower from white card, paint the centre and glue to the hat.*

▲ *Paint this charming pot with its humorous bow tie in bright, cheery patterns to complement your colour scheme.*

▶ *An ingenious clown's head attached to a wall displays a bushy fern doubling as a wild green hairstyle. A jaunty hat on a stick completes the effect.*

1 *Blow up a pear-shaped balloon to form a mould for the face. Mentally dividing the balloon in half lengthways and then again in half crossways, apply six layers of papier mâché to one of the resulting quarter sections at the rounded end of the balloon following the layered method on page 16. When the papier mâché has dried, separate it from the balloon and trim the edges level to make a neat shape for the head.*

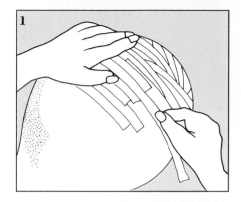

2 *Form a flat back to the head by holding the papier mâché against a piece of corrugated card and drawing around the edges to form a half circle. Cut out the back, cutting a straight edge across the diameter of the half circle. Cut two holes in the back 2.5 cm (1 in) below the straight edge and 5 cm (2 in) from the sides to allow the head to be hung on the wall.*

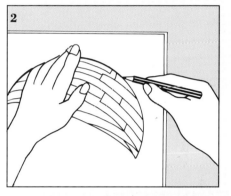

3 *Attach the back to the head using brown paper tape. Glue a polystyrene ball 4.5 cm (1¾ in) in diameter to the centre of the face as a nose. Apply another four layers of papier mâché to the head, trimming the upper edge level when the papier mâché has dried. Sand and fill the head (see page 19) and paint it white.*

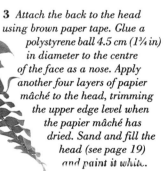

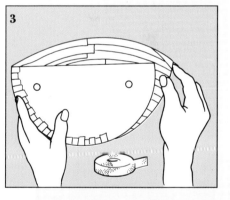

4 *Apply a thin layer of yellow paint to an old plate or tile. Dab at the paint with a damp sponge, then dab the paint lightly onto the face. Cut out template facial features from scrap paper and gently attach the features to the face with masking tape. Draw around the templates when you are happy with the design. Remove the templates and paint in the features.*

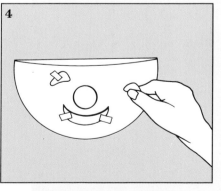

Plant Life

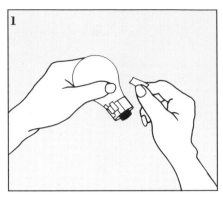

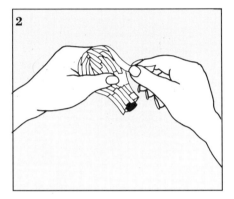

*Fill a balloon with air to create a
mould for the large hot-air
balloon. Use an old light bulb as a
mould for the small balloon. Wrap
a strip of thin card around the
neck of the bulb, overlapping the
ends; likewise with the balloon.
Stick the ends together with brown
paper tape. Smear petroleum jelly
over the bulb but take care to
avoid the card strip.*

1 *Adhere the card strip to the
moulds using pieces of newspaper
and PVA medium.*

2 *Apply four layers of papier
mâché to the moulds following the
layered method on page 16.*

◀ *Up, up and away with these flower-decked hot-air balloons. Fill plastic containers with vividly-coloured cut flowers, add water and place in the beribboned baskets. Hang the balloons in pride of place to brighten your home on dull days.*

3 Using a craft knife, slice the papier mâché on the bulb in half following the cut and rejoin method on page 18. Remove the bulb and rejoin the sections. Apply four more layers of papier mâché to the large and small balloons. Burst the balloon and remove it. Trim the edges level. Sand, fill and undercoat the balloons (see page 19).

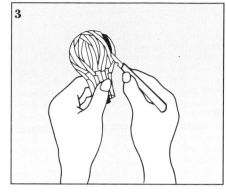

4 Cover the surface of the balloons with paint. Using a sponge, dab paint in a contrasting colour onto the balloons. Apply an additional colour to the lower band.

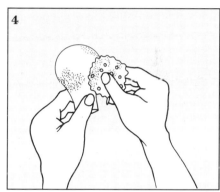

5 Cut assorted floral motifs from giftwrap and glue to the balloons with PVA medium. Varnish the balloons all over with PVA medium and leave to dry. Paint baskets in a matching colour.

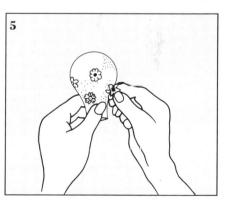

6 Pierce a hole in the top of each balloon. Knot the end of a length of narrow ribbon and thread upwards through the hole to fix to the ceiling. Divide the lower band of each balloon into quarters, pierce a hole at each division and thread with lengths of ribbon. Thread the ribbons between the weave of the basket and fasten the ends together in bows.

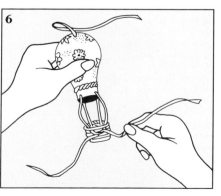

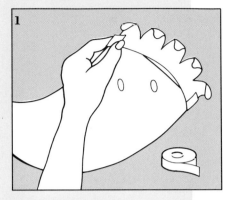

1 *Refer to the templates on page 107 to cut a base from corrugated card and a frill from thin card. Cut out the small circles on the base so that the cornucopia can be hung on the wall. Roll each scallop on the frill around a pencil to curve the points downwards. Use brown paper tape to attach the frill to the base, matching the dots on the frill to the corners of the cornucopia base.*

▶ *This stylish cornucopia of dried flowers would make a memorable gift for a special celebration. Paint on entwined monograms instead of the delicate fleur-de-lys motif to personalize a wedding or anniversary gift.*

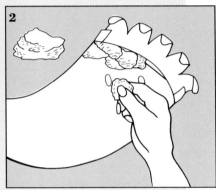

2 *Smear the upper side of the base with petroleum jelly. Do not apply petroleum jelly to the cut corrugated edges or the frill. Build up a mould for the cornucopia by pressing clay onto the base, smoothing the clay level with the straight edge of the frill and tapering towards the narrow end of the base. Spread clay on the 'tassel'. Indent the details on the tassel with a knife.*

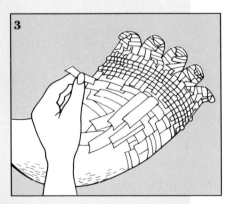

3 *Roll two narrow sausages of clay and lay them across the cornucopia, making sure they are level with the straight edge of the frill. Apply five layers of papier mâché following the layered method on page 16. Stick the papier mâché over the cut corrugated card edges and onto the back of the base. It is not necessary to cover the back of the base entirely.*

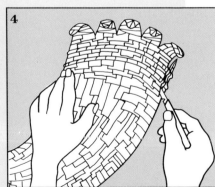

4 *Slice through the papier mâché and clay to just above the base. Remove the clay and rejoin the cut edges following the cut and rejoin method on page 18. Apply four more layers of papier mâché. Sand, fill and undercoat the model (see page 19). Paint the cornucopia with pink pearlized paint, highlighting the details with gold paint. Refer to the template on page 107 to paint the gold fleurs-de-lys.*

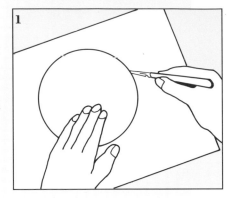

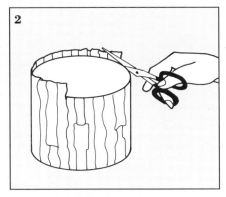

1 *To make the round jardinière,
cut a circle 17 cm (6¾ in) in
diameter from corrugated card for
the base and a strip of thin card
60 x 15 cm (24 x 6 in). For the
oval jardinière, cut an oval of
corrugated card 25 cm (10 in)
long and 20 cm (8 in) wide for the
base and a strip of thin card 85 x
17 cm (33½ x 6¾ in). Attach the
strips to their bases following the
card mould method on page 14.*

2 *Apply ten layers of papier mâché
to the jardinières following the
layered method on page 16,
extending the newspaper strips
above the upper edges. Trim the
upper edges level with the card.
Sand and undercoat the jardinière
(see page 19).*

▶ *These elegant stencilled
jardinières are based on
traditional papier-mâché designs.
Interesting and attractive
tortoiseshell and malachite effects
can be achieved by simply
sponging on paint.*

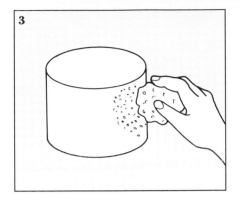

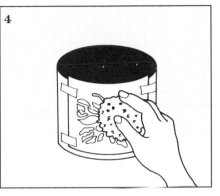

3 Use craft paint to apply a base colour to the outside of the jardinières – here, ochre was used for the round jardinière, green for the oval. Using a paintbrush, apply a thin film of paint to an old plate. Dab at the paint with a damp natural sponge, then dab the sponge over the base colour. The round jardinière was sponged with brick red, brown and black paint. A copper colour was sponged onto the oval jardinière.

4 Paint the inside and rim of both jardinières – black was used for the round jardinière and copper for the oval. Use the template on page 106 to trace the swag or butterfly onto stencil card. Cut away the cut-out areas and attach the stencil to the front of the jardinière with masking tape. Using a natural sponge, dab paint through the cut-out areas onto the jardinière. Varnish the jardinières with polyurethane varnish when the paint has dried.

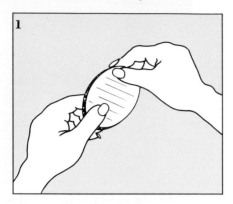

1 Draw four ovals on corrugated card for each section of the cactus. Add a short stalk approximately 2.5 cm (1 in) wide onto the largest oval to 'plant' in the pot. Cut out the card pieces with a craft knife. Squeeze all the cut edges to flatten them slightly, then glue the sections together holding each join in position until the glue dries.

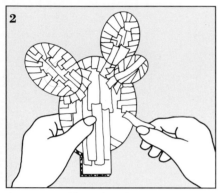

2 Apply five layers of papier mâché to the cactus following the layered method on page 16. It is not necessary to apply papier mâché to the stalk. Sand, fill and undercoat the model (see page 19), then apply green poster paint.

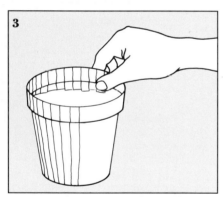

3 Apply two layers of papier mâché to a small plastic plant pot, gluing the ends of the newspaper strips to the underside of the base and inside the top of the pot. Apply a final layer using coloured papers.

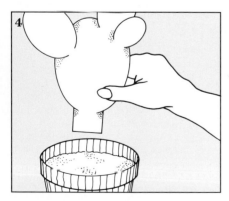

4 Prepare some quick-set cement and pour into the pot. Insert the cactus stalk into the cement before it sets hard. When the cement has hardened, glue some soil on top to cover. Trim the stalks from several cloves close to the clove heads and glue to the cactus.

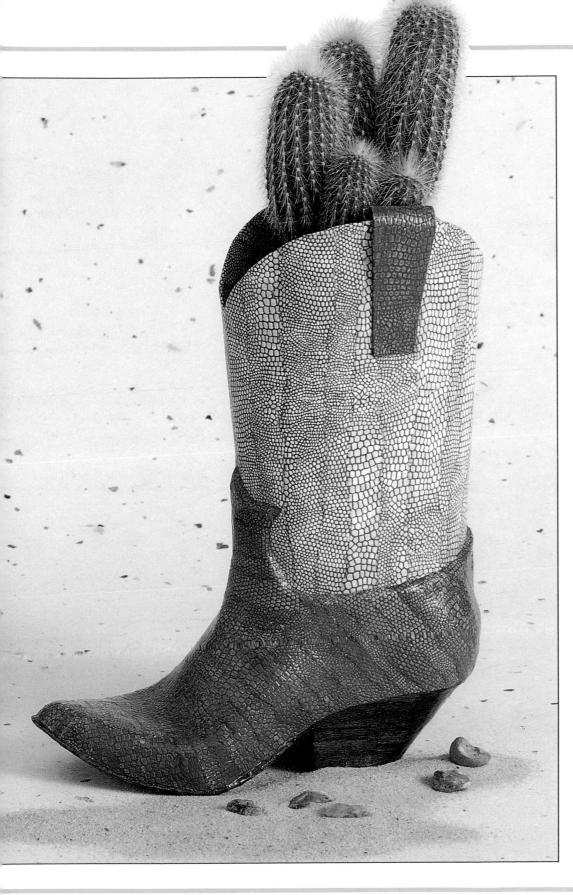

1 *Refer to the templates on pages 108 and 109 to cut a boot sole, heel base, heel side, boot upper and two pull straps from thin card. Score the heel base along the broken lines and fold at right angles along the scored line. Use the card mould method on page 14 to attach the shorter curved edge of the heel side to the curved edge of the heel base with brown paper tape. Tape the straight edges together.*

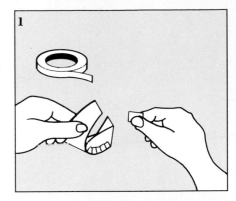

2 *Attach the heel to the curved end of the sole with brown paper tape. Bend the toe tip upwards. Bend the straight edges of the boot upper to meet edge to edge and stick together with brown tape. Smear the top of the sole and lower half of the boot upper with petroleum jelly. Breaking off small pieces at a time, press the clay to the sole, moulding it into the foot shape. Press the lower edge of the boot upper into the clay.*

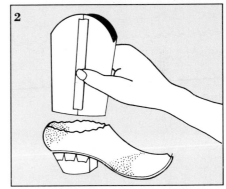

3 *Mould the clay over the lower edge of the boot upper shaping the decorative scalloped detail on the front. Apply four layers of papier mâché to the clay mould following the layered method on page 16. Remove the card sole and card boot upper and scoop out the clay. Tape the sole back in position and slip the boot upper back into the papier mâché.*

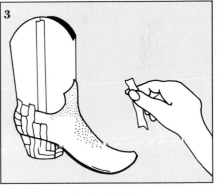

4 *Apply four more layers of papier mâché to the entire boot. Apply a final layer of wood-effect paper to the sole and heel and a layer of snakeskin-effect paper to the remainder of the boot, cutting the lower edges level with the sole. Bend the pull straps in half and cover with snakeskin-effect paper. Lightly paint the pull straps and the lower half of the boot a darker shade. Glue the pull straps to the sides of the boot.*

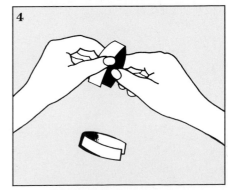

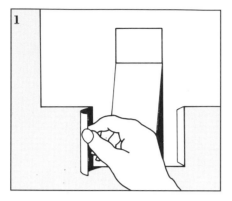

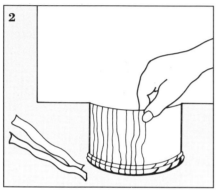

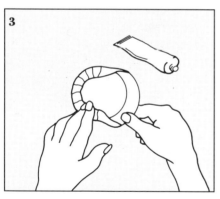

1 *Refer to the diagrams on page 109 to cut a tub from thin card and a background and stand from mounting board. Score the tabs on the stand and tub along the broken lines and bend them backwards. Glue the stand tab to the back of the background, making sure that the tab is centred and that the lower edges of the stand and background are level. Glue the back of the tub tabs to the back of the background so that the tub bows outwards at the front.*

2 *Glue two rows of cord along the lower edge of the tub, gluing the ends to the tabs at the back. Tear orange tissue paper into strips and apply to the tub and cord following the layered method on page 16. Glue the ends to the back of the tub. Using the template on page 110, cut eight leaves from green paper. Paint the veins, fold the leaves along the veins and open them out again.*

3 *Cut six 11 cm (4½ in) diameter circles of mounting board for flower centres. Scrunch up some tissue paper and glue on top to pad the centres. Cut six circles of brown textured paper 14 cm (5½ in) in diameter. Place the centres on the paper, tissue padding face downwards. Fold the paper over the edges of the circles and glue to the back of the flower centres.*

4 *Cut six strips of yellow crêpe paper 62.5 x 8 cm (25 x 3⅛ in). Divide each strip on the long side into twenty-five 2.5 cm (1 in) sections. Cut each section into a pointed petal, leaving a 1.5 cm (⅝ in) margin of paper along one edge in order not to separate the petals from each other. Glue the uncut long edge to the circumference of the flower centre, scrunching up the crêpe paper to fit. Arrange the leaves and flowers on the background. Glue in position, slightly bending the leaves outwards. Cut away the background around the sunflowers and leaves if it is visible from the front.*

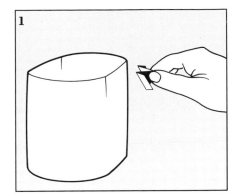

1 *Use a plastic container as a mould for the jug. A large salt carton was used for this model. Cut off the top of the container. Refer to the template on page 110 to cut a spout from thin card. Score along the broken lines, fold the tabs forward and, to form the spout, fold backwards along the centre scored line. Glue the tabs to the upper edge of the mould.*

◄ *This stunning display of sunflowers looks fabulous used as a firescreen throughout the summer. During the winter months, its dazzling colours will bring a warmth of their own into your home.*

▼ *Make use of broken china to create a pretty country-style mosaic jug and place a jam jar filled with freshly picked flowers inside.*

2 *From the mould, cut out the V shape within the spout. Cut a 1.5 cm (⅝ in) wide strip of thin card and glue the ends to the opposite side of the jug, bending the strip into a handle. Bind the handle with five layers of papier mâché following the layered method on page 16.*

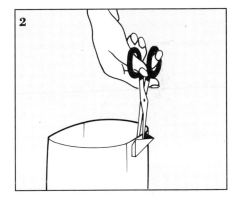

3 *Make up some pulp following the pulp method on page 17. Spread PVA medium on a section of the jug. Spread the pulp about 6 mm (¼ in) thick over the mould. Dab PVA medium onto the back of broken china pieces and press into the pulp. If you need to break china into small pieces, wrap the china in newspaper and smash with a hammer.*

4 *Use a knife to cover the edges of the china with pulp. Continue until the jug is covered with a mosaic of china. Leave to dry, then paint the pulp with cream emulsion or craft paint.*

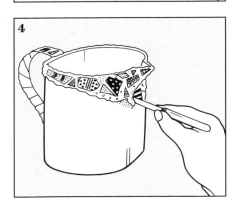

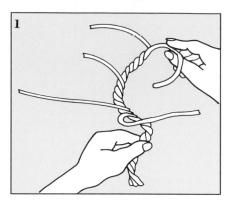

1 *Twist five lengths of thick wire together to form the tree trunk (bonsai wire from garden centres or suppliers is ideal). Splay out the wires to form branches. Bend the wires into an attractive shape. Add more branches by twisting the ends of finer wire around existing branches.*

2 *Following the manufacturer's directions, mix quick-set cement, available from hardware stores, in your chosen container. Insert the trunk before the cement sets hard.*

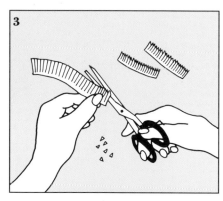

3 *To make the foliage, cut green paper strips 10 x 2.5 cm (4 x 1 in) and 6 x 1.5 cm (2½ x ⅝ in). Cut a fringe along one long edge. Carefully trim the ends of the fringe at an angle. Do not discard these tiny pieces – they may be useful later.*

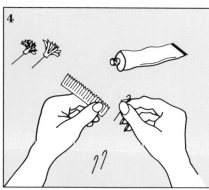

4 *Bend the end of a 6 cm (2½ in) length of fine wire into a hook. Slip the hook between the fringes at one end. Dab the long edge with glue. Coil this edge around the hook. Bind the wire around the branches. Cut tiny flowers from pink tissue paper using the template on page 110. Pierce a hole through the centre, cut a stamen string in half and thread one end through the hole. Glue the string around the branch wires. Coat the hardened cement with PVA medium. Tear a brown paper bag into small pieces and stick onto the PVA medium. Paint another bag with a watery solution of darker brown paint. When dry, tear this bag into strips about 5 mm (¼ in) 1 cm (⅝ in) wide.*

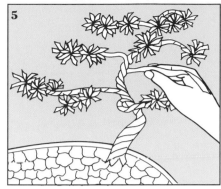

▼ *The traditional Japanese art of raising dwarf trees is recreated here with these delightful bonsai trees. Although usually very difficult to cultivate, as papier mâché models they will thrive forever.*

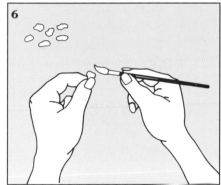

5 *Referring to the papier mâché layered method on page 16, apply the strips to the tree, binding them around the wires.*

6 *To make stones, screw up some brown paper and paint grey with gloss paint. To decorate the surface around the tree, either spread patches of PVA medium on the surface and trunk base and sprinkle on the tiny trimmed pieces from the foliage or glue a patch of green flock paper around the trunk. Glue stones around the trunk base.*

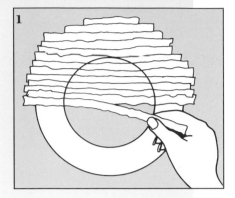

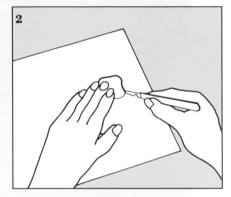

Smear the top of a plate with petroleum jelly. Apply eight layers of papier mâché following the layered method on page 16 with the ends of the newspaper strips extending beyond the plate rim. Trim the newspaper ends evenly around the rim. When dry, remove the plate mould. Sand and undercoat the plate (see page 19).

1 Apply narrow strips of torn coloured tissue with PVA medium, overlapping the plate rim. Stick the ends to the underside of the plate.

2 Cover the plate underside in the same way. For the pansy plate, use the template on page 110 to cut a pansy petal from thick card.

▼ *This pair of decorative pansy and plaid platters will enhance any room when hung on a wall. Once you have mastered the* *simple method of decorating the plates with coloured tissue paper, you can design your own pretty floral patterns.*

3 *Hold the template firmly on coloured tissue paper and lift the paper to tear it away around the edges of the template. Make three petals for each flower.*

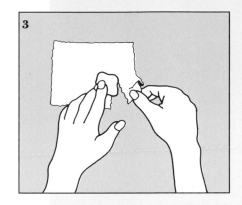

4 *Arrange the pansies on the plate. From tissue paper, tear by hand three black shapes and a small yellow circle for each pansy and some green leaves. Place the black shapes and yellow circles on the pansies with the leaves in-between.*

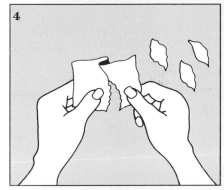

5 *For the plaid plate, hold a ruler firmly on coloured tissue paper and lift the paper against the ruler to tear a straight strip. Tear narrow strips and arrange them in a chequered pattern on the plate.*

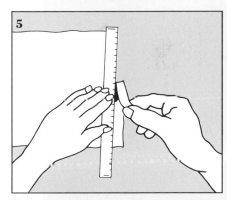

6 *When you are happy with the design, stick the tissue pieces in place with PVA solution. Apply three coats of PVA medium as a varnish, each time allowing the varnish to dry.*

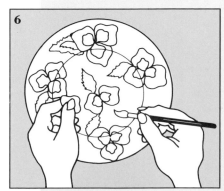

1 *Collect some fallen autumn leaves. Sandwich the leaves between kitchen paper towels or blotting paper, then slip them between the pages of a heavy book or press in a flower press. Leave for three weeks to press flat.*

▶ *This rustic bowl is decorated with attractive bronze-coloured fallen autumn leaves. An alternative summery effect can be achieved in the same way by using brightly-coloured pressed flowers.*

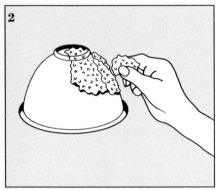

2 *Smear the outside of an upturned bowl with petroleum jelly, then apply a layer of papier mâché pulp about 6 mm (¼ in) thick to the surface following the pulp method on page 17.*

3 *Apply PVA medium to the back of the leaves and carefully press the leaves onto the pulp, smoothing them outwards from the centre. Set the bowl aside to dry. When the pulp has dried, remove the bowl mould and wipe out the petroleum jelly.*

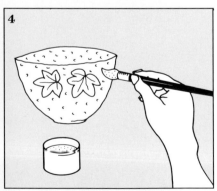

4 *Wipe the inside of the pulp bowl with a spirit such as lighter fuel to remove any remaining petroleum jelly. Paint the bowl with Indian inks, blending the colours together on the pulp. Apply five coats of polyurethane satin varnish to the whole surface of the bowl.*

Animal Antics

Animal lovers and fans of natural history will enjoy the
menagerie of popular pets and exotic creatures
in this chapter.

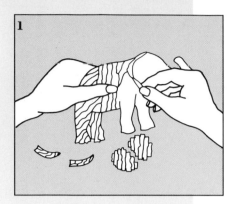

1 *Using a craft knife, cut away the tusks, ears and tail from a small plastic toy elephant. Discard the tail and smear the remaining pieces, including the body, with petroleum jelly. Apply papier mâché following the layered method on page 16, leaving foot soles and cut tusk ends uncovered. Apply strips to the outer sides of the ears only. Apply four layers to the elephant and six to the tusks and ears.*

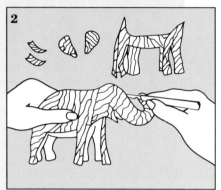

2 *When the papier mâché has dried, remove the plastic tusks and ears. Trim the papier mâché edges evenly. Using a craft knife, slice along the elephant from the base of the trunk down the front of each leg. From the tail position, slice down the back of each leg. On each side of the elephant, slice up the back of the front leg, along the underside, and down the back of the front leg. From the tail position, slice along the top of the elephant and along the upper and underside of the trunk, finishing at the base of the trunk.*

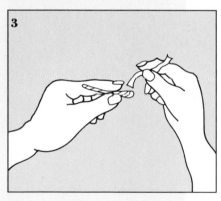

3 *Remove the three papier mâché sections from the plastic toy and join together with narrow strips of paper. Apply two more layers of papier mâché, then trim the feet level. For the tail, bind a length of string with narrow strips of newspaper. Sand the tusks (see page 19) and apply cream-coloured paint. Paint the elephant grey. When dry, glue the tusks in place.*

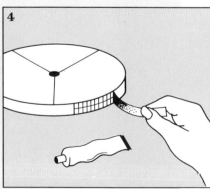

4 *Make two more elephants in the same way. Paint a pink halda and headdress on each elephant and decorate with beads, jewellery stones and tiny gold tassels applied with glue. Draw the eyes with a felt-tipped pen. Cut a hole 2 cm (¾ in) in diameter in the centre of a circular cake board 23 cm (9 in) in diameter. Cut a hole 1.5 cm (⅝ in) in diameter in the centre of a smaller cake board. Cover the large board with pink gummed paper, adding a gold paper strip around the side.*

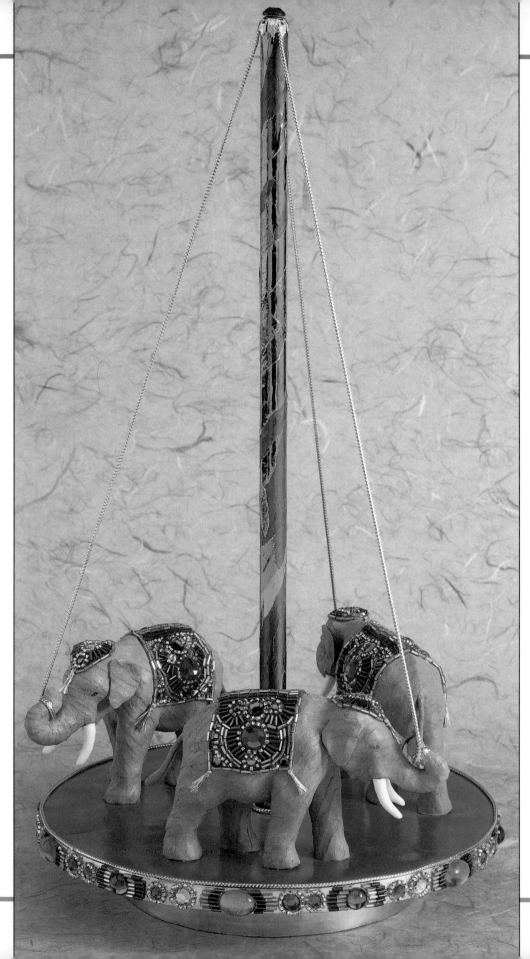

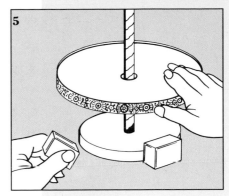

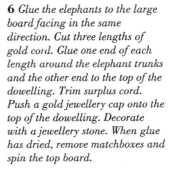

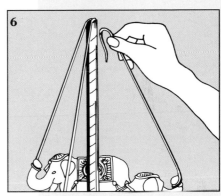

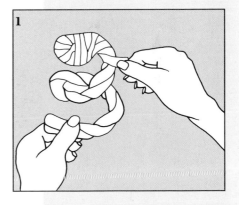

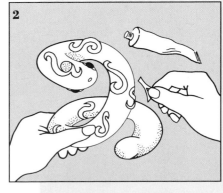

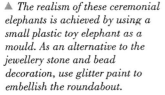

5 Decorate the side of the large board with jewellery stones and beads, then glue gold cord around the rim and the centre hole. Cover the small board with gold paper. Bind a length of wood dowelling 42 cm (16¾ in) long and 1.2 cm (½ in) wide with giftwrap. Place the dowelling upright in the centre hole of the small board. Lower the large board over the small board and dowelling and rest on three matchboxes positioned at intervals around the board.

6 Glue the elephants to the large board facing in the same direction. Cut three lengths of gold cord. Glue one end of each length around the elephant trunks and the other end to the top of the dowelling. Trim surplus cord. Push a gold jewellery cap onto the top of the dowelling. Decorate with a jewellery stone. When glue has dried, remove matchboxes and spin the top board.

1 To make the charmed snake, loosely twist together two thick pipe cleaners. Bend the ends at the top to form the head. Bend the snake into a coil, then apply four layers of papier mâché following the layered method on page 16, binding the newspaper strips around the pipe cleaners. Sand and undercoat the snake (see page 19).

2 Paint the snake with pearlized craft paint. Paint the eyes with gold paint, then glue jewellery stones to the top of the head and eyes. Decorate the snake with relief paint. Pierce a hole in the head for the tongue. Cut a forked tongue from thin pink card. Dab glue onto the tongue end and insert into the hole.

▲ *The realism of these ceremonial elephants is achieved by using a small plastic toy elephant as a mould. As an alternative to the jewellery stone and bead decoration, use glitter paint to embellish the roundabout.*

▶ *This charmed snake is fun and easy to make and can be decorated to great effect with relief paints and jewellery stones.*

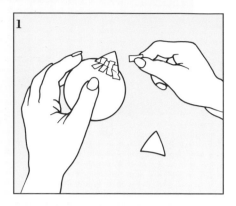

1 *To make the cats, cut two ears from thin card and attach to each side of a polystyrene ball with strips of newspaper and PVA medium. Cover the ball with papier mâché pulp following the pulp method on page 17. Roll two balls of pulp for the muzzle, flatten and press onto the ball.*

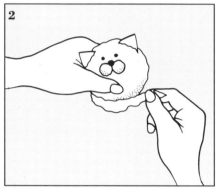

2 *Dab three black beads with PVA medium and press into the pulp as eyes and a nose. Roll a sausage of pulp for the tail and drape around the cat to balance it. Leave to dry, then paint the model.*

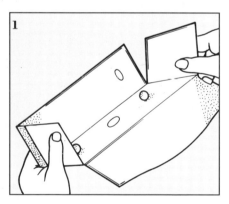

1 *To make the rocking mole, refer to the templates on page 110. Cut one mole box, two rocker ovals, one cone and two hands from thin card. Cut out the holes and score along the broken lines on the box and hands. Glue a bead 1.5 cm (⅝ in) wide onto the base at the dots. Fold the front, back and sides upwards and stick together with brown paper tape. Cut a strip of thin card measuring 34.5 x 5 cm (13½ x 2 in).*

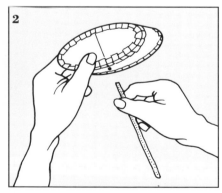

2 *Mark the centre on the ovals. Attach the strip of card to the two ovals with brown paper tape following the card mould method on page 14. Pierce a hole in the centre of the strip on the underside aligned with the centre of the ovals. Push the end of a thick pipe cleaner into the hole, glue in place and bend into a wriggling worm shape. Trim the end to a point.*

◀ *These comical, well-fed cats are very simple to make. Paint one to resemble a favourite feline friend.*

▼ *This burrowing mole will rock from side to side when the wriggling worm is rocked. There are two holes on the back of the box so that the model can be hung on a wall.*

3 *To make the worm's head, bend an 8 cm (3¼ in) length of pipe cleaner into thirds. Glue to the box front in line with the hole in the base. Bend the head downwards. Secure the worm head in position with strips of newspaper and PVA medium. To make the mole, overlap the straight edges of the cone and glue together. Glue to a polystyrene ball 6.5 cm (2½ in) in diameter. Glue the ball to the top of the rocker with the cone facing forwards.*

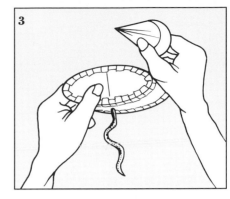

4 *Bend the hand tabs and fingers backwards. Apply three layers of papier mâché to the hands (but not the tabs), rocker and worm following the layered method on page 16. Glue the hand tabs to each side of the mole. Following the pulp method on page 16, apply papier mâché pulp to the box front, base and sides as well as to the mole head, covering the hand tabs.*

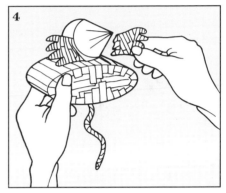

5 *Build up the cone point with more pulp. Dab the prongs of a toy-making nose and two small eyes with PVA medium. Insert the nose into the point of the cone with the eyes either side. Blend more pulp around the nose. With a thick needle, pierce three holes at each side of the nose to hold some whiskers. Leave to harden.*

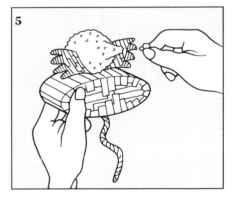

6 *Paint the worm with pearlized paint and the rest of the model with craft paints. Dab glue onto the end of several toy-making whiskers and insert in bunches into the holes. Slip the worm down through the hole in the box base.*

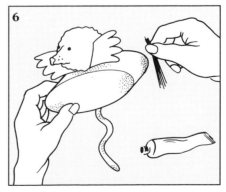

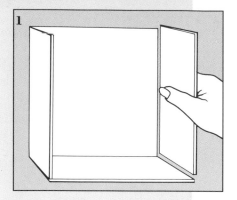

1 *To make the cupboard, use corrugated card 4 mm (⁵⁄₃₂ in) thick to cut one 14 x 14 cm (5½ x 5½ in) square for the back, two rectangles 14 x 6 cm (5½ x 2⅜ in) for the base and roof and two rectangles 14 cm x 5.6 cm (5½ x 2³⁄₁₆ in) for the sides. Glue the back upright on one long edge of the base, then glue the sides upright against the back on the short edges of the base.*

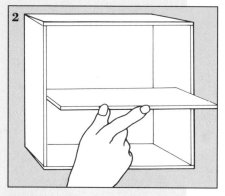

2 *Glue the roof on top of the back and sides. Cut one rectangle of corrugated card 13.2 x 5.6 cm (5³⁄₁₆ x 2³⁄₁₆ in) for the shelf. Glue the shelf inside the cupboard half-way between the roof and the base. Cut four doors and one pediment from corrugated card using the templates on page 111. Glue the doors together in pairs to make them thicker. Glue the pediment on top of the cupboard.*

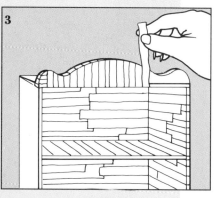

3 *Apply three layers of papier mâché to the cupboard and doors following the layered method on page 16. Apply a final layer of coloured paper, using a contrasting colour for the inside of the cupboard doors.*

4 *Referring to the templates on page 111, cut the motifs for the doors and pediment from coloured paper. Glue in position with PVA medium. Cut out motifs for the sides of the cupboard and inside of the doors and stick in place. Give the cupboard and doors a final coat of PVA medium to seal the motifs. Leave to dry.*

▲ *The doors on this exquisitely decorated cupboard open to reveal a pair of cunning crocodiles.*

5 *Glue two tiny hinges on the outer edges of the doors. Snip moulding pins 4 mm (⁵⁄₃₂ in) long with wire cutters. Dab glue on the ends and insert into the doors through the hinge holes. Place the doors against the cupboard and glue the hinges to the cupboard. Secure with moulding pins as before. Fasten the doors with a swing hook and screw-eye, snipping off the ends of the screws inside the doors with wire cutters. Dab gold paint on the pin heads.*

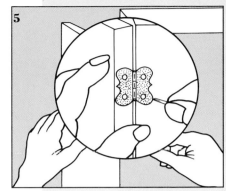

6 *Use the templates on page 111 to make the crocodiles. Cut two crocodile bodies from corrugated card using the yellow crocodile template. Then draw – but do not cut out – a pair of crocodiles on paper. Place the corrugated card bodies on the drawings. Press the ends of the bodies along the broken lines to flatten these edges slightly.*

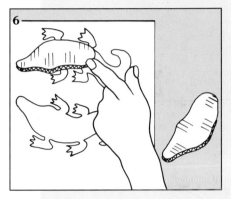

7 *Smear the crocodiles with petroleum jelly. Following the pulp method on page 17, apply papier mâché pulp to the corrugated card bodies and then onto the feet and tail within the drawing outline. Build up the pulp on top of the crocodile bodies.*

8 *Dab two beads with PVA medium and press them into the pulp as eyes. Carefully spread a little pulp over the eyes as eyelids. Leave to harden, then lift the crocodiles off the drawing and card. Apply some more pulp on the underside of the crocodile bodies to fatten them. Leave to dry, then paint the crocodiles with Indian inks.*

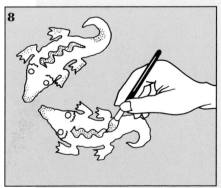

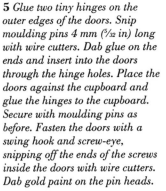

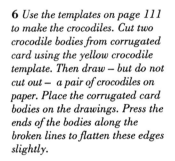

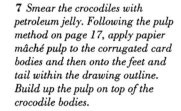

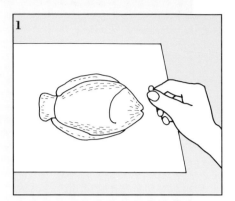

1 *Use the templates on page 112 to trace the fish onto paper. Using plastic clay, mould the fish within the outlines of the drawing – you can make the design as simple or as intricate as you wish by adding separate fins and a ball of clay for the eye. Smear the top of the fish with petroleum jelly. Apply six layers of papier mâché following the layered method on page 16.*

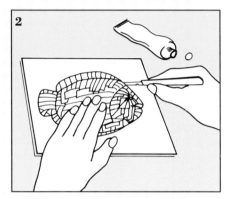

2 *Remove the clay mould and trim the edges of the fish level. Spread glue on the cut edges and press onto thick card. Cut around the fish with a craft knife. Sand and undercoat the fish (see page 19), then paint with Indian inks. Cut two rectangles of mounting board (four-sheet thickness) 14 x 10 cm (5½ x 4 in) for the front and back of the frame.*

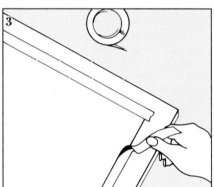

3 *Cut a window in the front frame 11 x 7 cm (4¼ x 2¾ in). Paint a design onto the front frame with Indian inks. Paint the cut edges of the window. Cut a rectangle of acetate 13 x 9 cm (5 x 3½ in) and glue behind the window. The frame is lined with painted watercolour paper. To stretch the paper before painting, tape the edges to a piece of wood or thick card. Dampen the paper and leave to dry.*

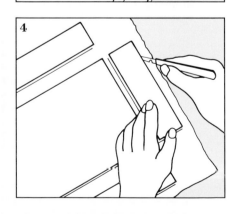

4 *Paint the paper with Indian inks, blending the colours together while the paint is still wet. Cut two strips of four-sheet thickness mounting board 14 x 3 cm (5½ x 1¼ in) for the top and bottom of the frame and two strips 9.7 x 3 cm (3⅞ x 1¼ in) for the sides. Carefully untape the watercolour paper from the piece of wood or card and place painted side down. Using spray adhesive, stick the mounting board strips and back frame to the paper. Trim the paper level with the edges of the mounting board pieces.*

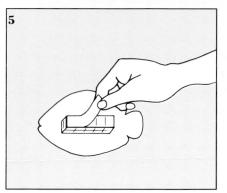

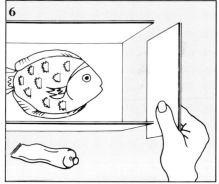

5 Apply two layers of foam adhesive strip to the back of the fish and stick the fish centrally to the back frame.

6 Glue the top and bottom mounting board pieces upright along the long edges of the back frame, then glue the sides upright along the short edges. Glue the front frame on top and a picture hanger to the back. Paint the top, bottom and sides of the frame.

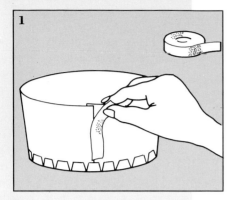

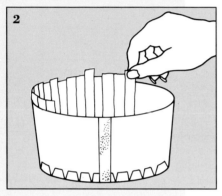

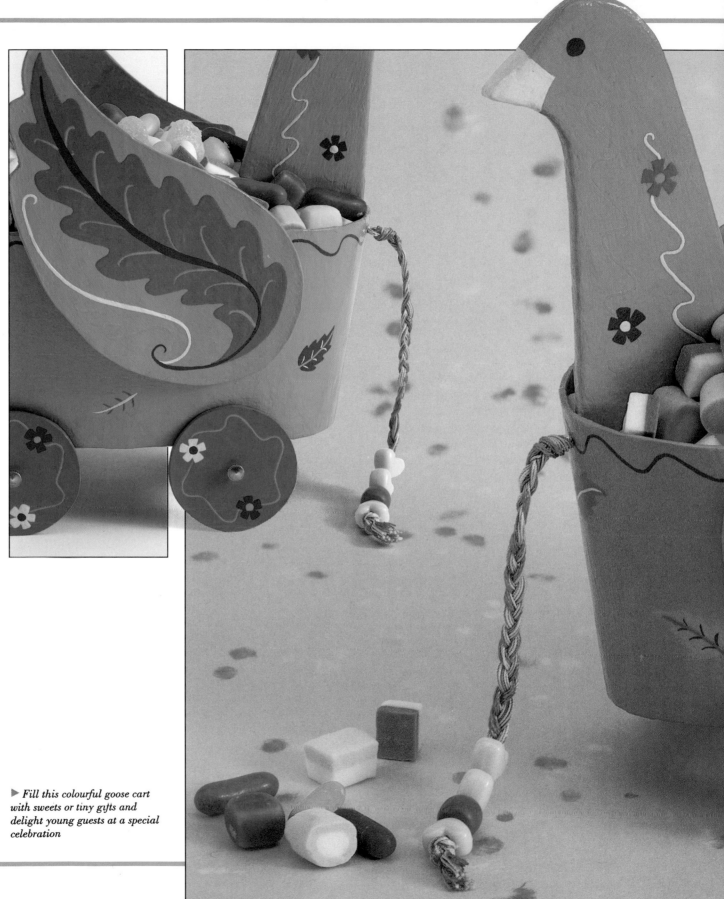

Use the templates on pages 112-113 to cut a cart base, side and two wings from thin card. Cut a head from corrugated card. Matching the dots, attach the lower edge of the cart side to the base following the card mould method on page 14.

1 Stick the overlapped ends of the cart side together with brown paper tape.

2 Apply four layers of papier mâché to the inside of the cart following the layered method on page 16.

▶ Fill this colourful goose cart with sweets or tiny gifts and delight young guests at a special celebration

3 Trim the papier mâché level with the top of the cart. Saw wood dowelling 1.2 cm (½ in) in diameter into two 8 cm (3¼ in) lengths and glue to the cart base along the axle lines. Apply four layers of papier mâché to the outside surface of the cart and trim the papier mâché to the level of the cart.

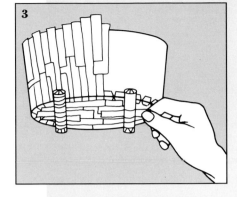

4 Cover the goose head with four layers of papier mâché. Glue the head upright inside the front of the cart and secure in place with strips of newspaper and PVA medium. Apply four layers of papier mâché to each side of the wings. Trim the papier mâché level with the card edges. Sand and fill the cart and wings (see page 19). Glue the wings to the sides of the cart and undercoat the entire model.

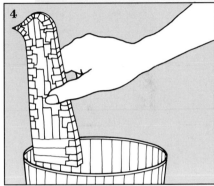

5 From mounting board cut four circles 4.5 cm (1¾ in) in diameter for the wheels. Paint the cart and wheels with craft paints, copying the pattern on the templates and adding tiny leaves and flowers to the cart and wheels. Alternatively, create your own design. Push a map pin, available from stationers and craft suppliers, into the end of each axle to make a hole, then pierce a hole through the centre of the wheels. Make the holes large enough to spin the wheel on the pin. Insert the pins through the wheels into the axles.

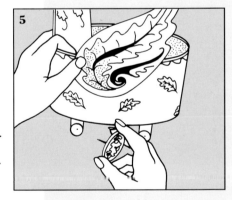

6 Screw a screw-eye through the front of the cart and into the neck. Thread with embroidery threads and plait together. Thread on a few colourful beads, then knot the ends together.

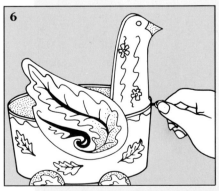

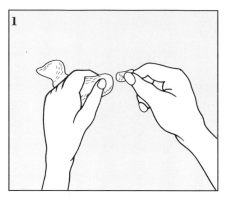

1 *To make the hare, mould an oval of clay 7.5 cm (3 in) long for the body and bend the ends upwards. Mould a pear shape for the head 4 cm (1½ in) long and press the head to the end of the body, blending the clay with a finger. Mould a small pear shape for the tail and press to the end of the body.*

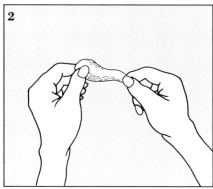

2 *Roll four sausages of clay for legs. Flatten one end of each leg a little to form thighs. Squeeze the lower front legs to make them thinner and squash the ends of the legs to form paws. For the back legs, bend the lower third of each leg downwards at an angle. Press the legs to each side of the upturned oval, blending the clay into the body.*

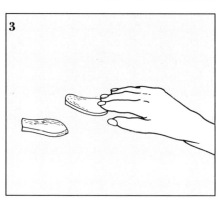
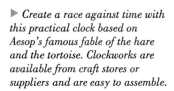

3 *Roll out a lump of clay to a thickness of 6 mm (¼ in) and cut two ears 5 cm (2 in) long. Pat the edges along the ears to curve them and bend the ends of the ears upwards.*

▶ *Create a race against time with this practical clock based on Aesop's famous fable of the hare and the tortoise. Clockworks are available from craft stores or suppliers and are easy to assemble.*

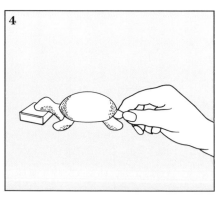

4 *To make the tortoise, mould an oval of clay for the shell 7 cm (2¾ in) long. Flatten the underside of the shell to about 3 cm (1¼ in) thick. Mould a pear shape for the head and stretch the wide end outwards to form a neck. Press the end of the neck under one end of the shell and support the head on a small box. Roll five short sausages of clay for legs and a tail and press them under the body. Pinch the tail to a point at the end.*

5 *Smear the models with petroleum jelly. Following the layered method on page 16, apply five layers of papier mâché, including to the top of the hare's ears. When dry, slice through the papier mâché with a craft knife, cutting along the underside and along the head and tail.*

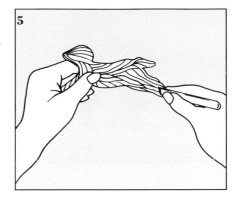

6 *Scoop out the clay and rejoin the cut edges using the cut and rejoin method on page 18. Apply two more layers of papier mâché then a final layer using appropriately coloured paper. Trim the edges of the hare's ears level, apply a layer of coloured paper then glue to the back of the hare's head. Reinforce the join with more coloured paper. Paint in the facial features.*

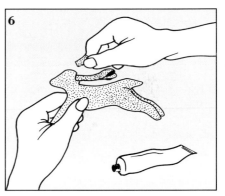

7 *Using the templates on page 113, cut two clocks from corrugated card and numerals and dots from paper. Cut a strip of thin card 64 x 8 cm (25¼ x 3¼ in). Cut out the hole on one clock for the clock hands. Attach the strip between the clocks with brown paper tape following the card mould method on page 110. Apply two layers of papier mâché to the clock, sticking the newspaper ends to the inside. Apply a final layer of green textured paper.*

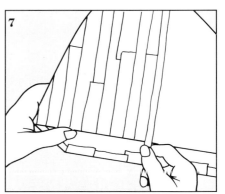

8 *Recut the hole and paint the clock hands. Glue the numerals and dots in place. Attach the clockwork and hands. Glue the tortoise to the clock. Pierce a hole at the end of each of the hare's hind legs and hold the hare on the clock in a leaping pose. Mark the positions of the holes and pierce holes at the marks. Insert a 7 cm (2¾ in) length of wire into each leg then into the clock holes, bending the wire against the inside of the clock. Glue in place. Cut several flowers from yellow paper using the template on page 110. Thread stamen strings through holes in the centre of the flowers. Pierce holes on the clock, dab the string ends with glue and insert through the holes.*

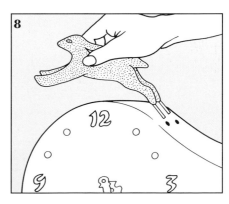

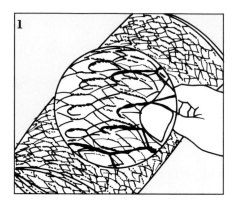

1 *To make the legs of the dinosaur, cut four rectangles of chicken wire 10 x 7 cm (4 x 2¾ in). Bend into tubes with the short ends meeting. Twist the cut ends together using pliers or your fingers. Cut a rectangle of chicken wire 33 x 29 cm (13 x 11½ in) for the body and bend into a tube with the long ends meeting. Twist the cut ends together.*

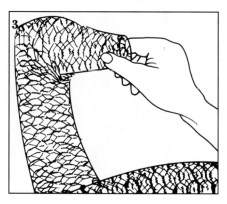

2 *Position the legs under the body and fix in place by hooking the cut ends from the legs onto the wire of the body. Squeeze the ends of the body at the sides to make it oval in shape. Cut two strips of chicken wire 30 x 14 cm (12 x 5¾ in) for the neck and tail. Bend into long tubes, bringing together long edges, and twist the cut wires together. Fix in position at both ends of the body by hooking the cut ends of the tubes to the rim of the body tube.*

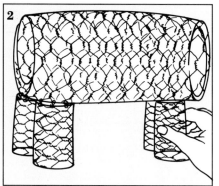

3 *Bend the neck upwards, then bend over the body to form the head. Squeeze the top and bottom of the head to flatten it slightly. Bend the tail around the side of the body and squeeze it to form a tapering tip. When you are happy with the shape, apply a layer of papier mâché following the layered method on page 16.*

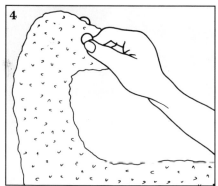

4 *Apply papier mâché pulp to the model, following the pulp method on page 17. Press two beads to the top of the head as eyes and make an indent in the papier mâché pulp with a thick needle to form a mouth.*

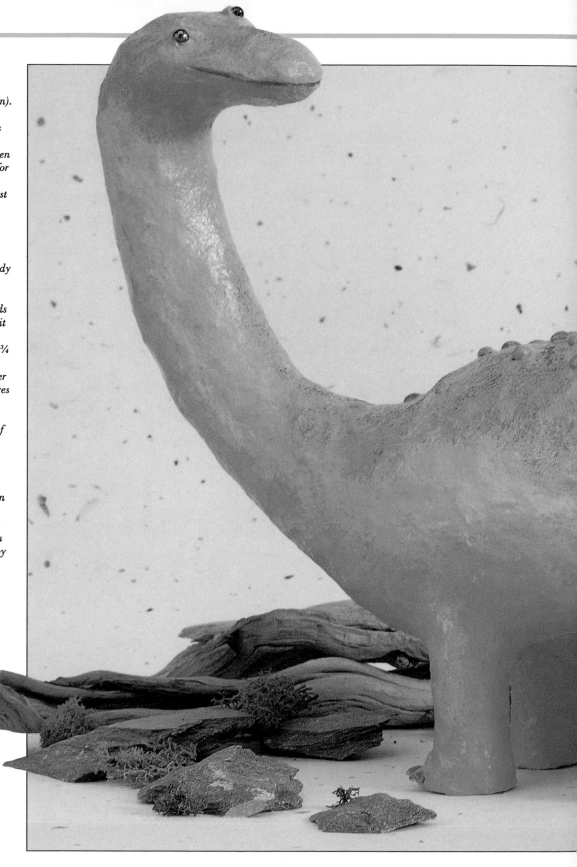

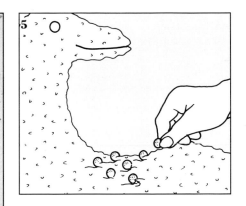

5 *Dab PVA medium on the top of the body and on the front of the feet. Press split peas into the PVA medium to suggest raised markings on top of the body and toes on the feet.*

6 *Leave to dry. Paint the model, then dab on contrasting coloured paint with a sponge.*

◀ *This dashing diplodocus dinosaur is moulded over chicken wire. The pliable nature of this wire makes it easy to shape into a variety of creatures.*

Top Tables

Create the feel of a country kitchen with everlasting fruits and vegetables or enhance your table with practical models and beautiful trimmings.

1 Smear the outside of an upturned oval glass or plastic bowl with petroleum jelly. Apply eight layers of papier mâché to the outside following the layered method on page 16. If the bowl has a rim, do not cover with papier mâché. When dry, remove the papier mâché from the mould. Trim the papier mâché edge level.

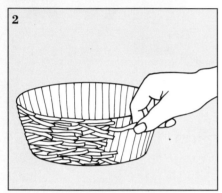

2 Paste together four layers of newspaper with PVA solution. Leave to dry, then cut into strips 3 mm (⅛ in) wide and 9 cm (3½ in) long. Attach the strips to the outside of the papier mâché bowl with PVA solution, overlapping them at random to create a nest-like effect.

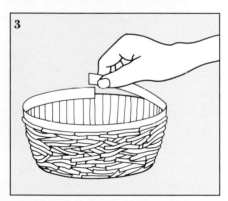

3 Cut a strip of thin card 1.5 cm (⅝ in) wide and 2 cm (¾ in) longer than the circumference of the bowl. Wrap the strip around the inside top of the bowl with 6 mm (¼ in) extending above the rim. Overlap the end of the strip. Apply three layers of papier mâché inside the bowl, securing the strip of card in place. Trim the papier mâché level with the upper edge of the strip.

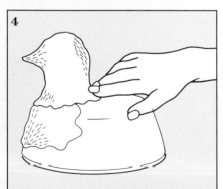

4 Collect pictures of hens from books and magazines to refer to when moulding and painting the hen. With the glass or plastic bowl mould upside down, build one end outwards with clay to form the hen's chest. Mould a head and beak from clay and position on the bowl. Smooth the edges of the clay onto the bowl. Smear the bowl and clay with petroleum jelly, then apply ten layers of papier mâché. If the bowl has a rim, do not cover with papier mâché.

5 *Slip the hen off the mould and trim the lower edge level. Refer to the templates on page 114 to cut a comb, two jowls, two wings, one tail and approximately ten feathers from thin card. You may wish to enlarge or reduce the size of these pieces to match the proportions of your hen; the hen pictured here is 19 cm (7½ in) long. Cut the lower edge of the comb to fit the shape of the head. Attach the comb to the top of the head and the jowls below the beak with strips of newspaper and PVA medium.*

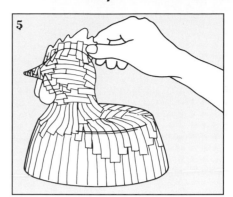

6 *Pull the wings and tail between thumb and forefinger to curve. Attach the wings to each side of the hen and the tail to the back of the bird with strips of newspaper and PVA medium. Bend the tail tip downwards.*

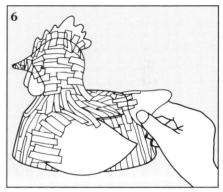

7 *Pull the rounded ends of the feathers betweeen thumb and forefinger to curve. Apply five layers of papier mâché to one side of the feathers, wings and tail leaving the newspaper ends extending over the ends of the card. Trim the papier mâché level with the wing and tail card. Trim all edges of the feathers.*

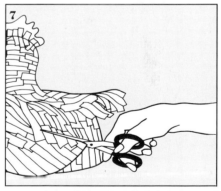

8 *Attach the feathers around the hen's neck with strips of newspaper and PVA medium, cutting the straight ends shorter on the front and back feathers. Add more feathers if necessary. Sand and fill the hen when dry (see page 19). Undercoat the hen and nest inside and out. Use acrylic paints to paint the nest yellow ochre. Paint the hen and when dry, apply two coats of polyurethane satin varnish to the whole model.*

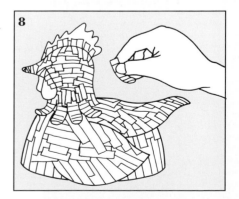

1 *To make the red and green peppers and the carrots, smear real vegetables with petroleum jelly. Apply five layers of papier mâché following the layered method on page 16. Slice the papier mâché around the centre of each vegetable following the cut and rejoin method on page 18. Remove the moulds and rejoin the sections. Apply a further three layers of papier mâché. Sand, fill and undercoat the vegetables (see page 19). If you wish, glue fine raffia to the top of the carrots and paint green. Paint the peppers with glossy craft paint and the carrots with orange poster paint.*

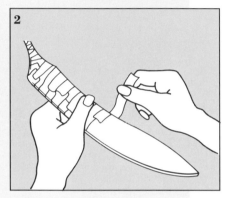

2 *From corrugated card, cut a runner bean shape approximately 28 cm (11 in) in length. Cover with four layers of papier mâché following the layered method on page 16. Sand, fill and undercoat the bean, then paint with green poster paint.*

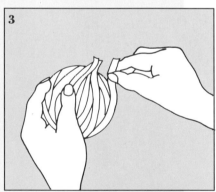

3 *To make an onion, cover a polystyrene ball 6.5 cm (2½ in) in diameter with two layers of papier mâché following the layered method on page 16 and using strips of newspaper about 6 mm (¼ in) wide. Leave a few strips of newspaper extending at the top of the ball. Paint the onion with a weak and a strong solution of ochre Indian ink. Dab glue onto the onion base and press lengths of fine raffia onto the glue. Trim the raffia ends and paint to match the colour of the onion.*

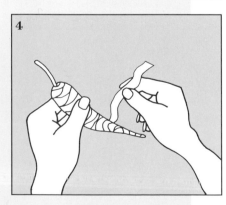

4 *To make a chilli pepper, cut a length of string 13.5 cm (5½ in) long. Bind with strips of newspaper following the layered method on page 16 starting approximately 3.5 cm (1½ in) from one end of the string. The uncovered portion will form the stalk. Build up a thicker layer of paper at one end to create a realistic shape. Taper the papier mâché towards the end of the string, bending the string in a gentle curve as you work.*

▶ *These realistic vegetables are displayed to great effect in a rustic basket lined with straw. The models are moulded over real vegetables or constructed from a polystyrene ball or cardboard.*

5 *Sand, fill and undercoat the chilli pepper (see page 19). Paint with glossy craft paints.*

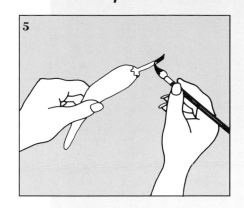

6 *To make a leek, take the cardboard tube from the inside of a roll of kitchen paper towels. Cover the open ends of the tube with newspaper strips and PVA solution. Bind strips of newspaper around one end to make a bulbous shape. Cover the entire tube with two layers of papier mâché following the layered method on page 16.*

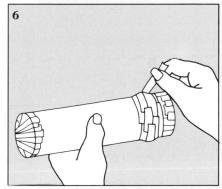

7 *Cut eight strips of newspaper 26 x 11 cm (10¼ x 4½ in). Paste the strips together in pairs with PVA medium to form the leaves. Wrap the leaves around the tube overlapping the long edges and extending each leaf beyond the top of the tube by approximately 9.5 cm (3¾ in).*

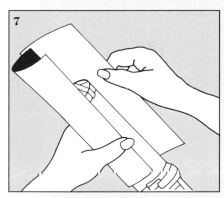

8 *Cut down the centre of each leaf to the top of the tube. Gently sand the leek where the leaves join the tube (see page 19). Carefully peel down the outer leaves and undercoat the inner leaves. Leave to dry, then undercoat the next layer. Continue until the entire leek and its leaves have been undercoated. Paint with Indian inks, blending green paint at the leaf end of the leek into cream at the base.*

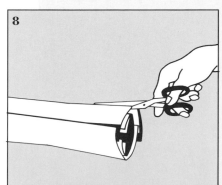

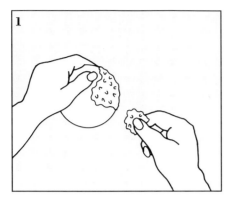

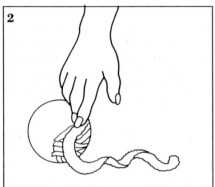

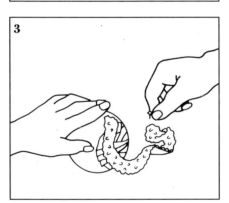

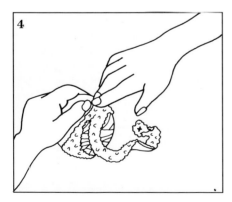

1 *Following the pulp method on page 17, cover a polystyrene ball with pulp to make an orange or lemon. Build up the pulp at each end of the lemon and mould into a realistic shape. Carefully remove the seed from a clove, then press the clove into one pointed end of the lemon, or into the base of the orange. Set fruit aside to harden. Add more pulp if necessary. Paint with craft paints. Apply a touch of green paint to the clove on the lemon.*

2 *To make a half-peeled orange, cover a section of a polystyrene ball with two layers of papier mâché following the layered method on page 16. From thick paper, such as wallpaper lining paper, tear a circle roughly the size of the papier mâché-covered area on the ball. Tear the circle into a spiral in the same way as a peeled orange rind. Using PVA medium, glue one end of the spiral to the ball at the edge of the papier mâché.*

3 *Cover the outside of the spiral with pulp following the pulp method on page 17. Gently arrange the spiral into an attractive shape. Remove the seed from a clove, trim the stalk then press the clove into the pulp at the end of the spiral. Leave to dry.*

4 *Apply papier mâché pulp to the area of the ball not covered with layered papier mâché. When dry, paint the pulp orange and the remainder cream.*

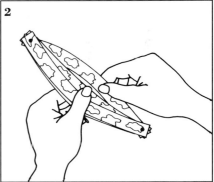

To make a bowl, cut six strips of thin card 30 x 2.5 cm (12 x 1 in). Tear gummed paper into strips or uneven shapes. Dampen the pieces and stick to both sides of the strips.

1 Make a hole at each end of the strips with a hole punch. Apply five coats of PVA medium as a varnish. Leave to dry.

2 Fasten the strips together at each end with brass paper fasteners. Pull the strips apart to form a bowl shape.

▲ With these dramatic and everlasting citrus fruits displayed in abstract-patterned bowls, vibrant colours and simple shapes combine to evoke a hot and sultry summer mood.

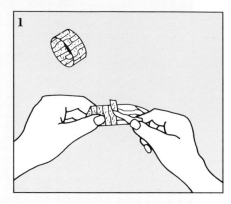

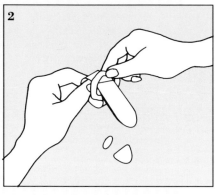

▶ *Break for the border with this Wild West breakfast setting. The amusing sombreros can hold place name cards and the bright napkins are fastened with cowboy belts. Even the egg cups are wearing neckerchiefs!*

To make a napkin ring, cut a slice 3 cm (1¼ in) wide from a kitchen paper towel inner tube. Refer to the templates on page 114 to cut a belt, tip, buckle and prong from thin card. Apply four layers of papier mâché to these pieces and to the tube following the layered method on page 16. Stick the ends of the strips to the inside of the ring.

1 *Apply a final layer of papier mâché using textured paper on the ring and belt and silver paper on the remaining pieces.*

2 *Paint the ring and belt. Glue the end of the belt onto the ring. Slip the buckle over the join. Glue the prong to overlap the buckle and belt. Glue the tip to the end of the belt.*

1 *To make an egg cup, cut a slice from a kitchen paper towel inner tube 5 cm (2 in) wide. Cover with four layers of papier mâché following the layered method on page 16, sticking the ends of the strips to the inside of the tube. Refer to the templates on page 114 to cut a neckerchief and tail from blotting paper. Lightly dampen the pieces using a paintbrush.*

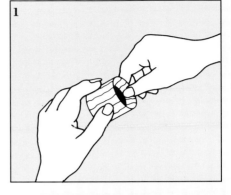

2 *Making a pleat in the lower end of the neckerchief, wrap it around the tube and stick in place with PVA medium. Make a small pleat at the centre of the tail and stick to the neckerchief ends with PVA medium. Cut a circle 2.5 cm (1 in) in diameter from blotting paper, dampen and turn under the edges. Stick over the tail pleat to form a knot. When dry, coat with PVA medium. Allow to dry, then cover the neckerchief with four layers of papier mâché following the layered method on page 16.*

3 *To make a sombrero, flatten a ball of clay and lift the edge of the clay circle upwards to form a hat brim. Mould an oval of clay for the crown. Cut one end of the clay oval straight. Press the crown to the brim centre. Smear the sombrero with petroleum jelly, then apply papier mâché pulp to the mould on the upperside following the pulp method on page 17. Using a thick needle, pierce holes around the brim's rim.*

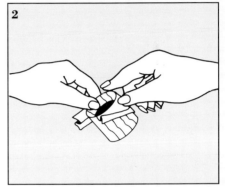

4 *Set the sombrero aside to dry. Remove the clay mould and paint the hat. Thread embroidery yarn through the holes. Glue ric-rac braid around the crown. Write a child's or a guest's name on coloured card and slip behind the ric-rac.*

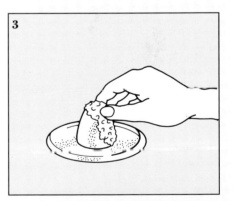

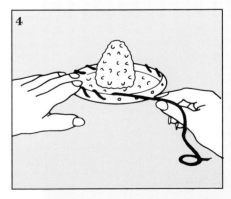

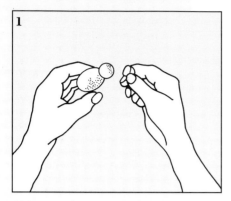

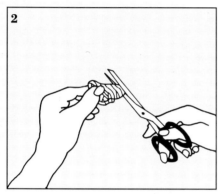

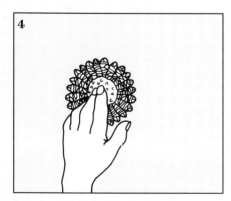

1 *For the bumble bee, mould a clay oval for the abdomen and two balls for the thorax and head. Press the thorax to the abdomen. Cut the head in half and press one half onto the thorax.*

2 *Roll out a piece of clay to a thickness of 6 mm (¼ in). Use the template on page 114 to cut a pair of clay wings. Pat the edges to curve them. Smear the clay pieces with petroleum jelly. Following the layered method on page 16, apply six layers of papier mâché to the moulds, but not to the wing undersides. Cut a flat oval from the underside of the bee with a craft knife. Remove clay from all parts and trim wing edges level. Spread glue on the flat underside of the bee and press onto thick card. Cut away the card around the bee. Sand and undercoat the pieces (see page 19). Paint with Indian inks. Glue wings in place and attach a fridge magnet to the bee's underside.*

3 *For the sunflower, roll out clay to a thickness of 7 mm (⁵⁄₁₆ in). Use the template on page 114 to cut out a sunflower from the clay. Make indentations along the solid lines with a knife. Pat the cut edges to curve them. Press the centre to flatten a little. Smear the model with petroleum jelly. Apply six layers of papier mâché to one side of the model, following the layered method on page 16.*

4 *When dry, remove the clay and trim the edges of the petals. Pierce a hole at either side of the flower. Roll a ball of pulp following the pulp method on page 17. Spread PVA medium onto the sunflower centre. Flatten the ball and press to the centre. Leave to dry. Paint the model. When dry, thread cord through the holes and tie around the neck of a bottle.*

▼ *Make edible gifts extra special by adding exquisite papier mâché decorations. The bumble bee on the honey jar is a fridge magnet. The cheery sunflower trimming the bottle of olive and sunflower oil can be hung on a wall when the oil has been used up. The jar of preserved fruit decorated with golden pears can be reused to hold keepsakes.*

► *This charming Christmas table centrepiece of a partridge in a pear tree can easily be adapted to make alternative seasonal trees, for instance a brightly-painted exotic bird crowning a tree of glossy red apples.*

1 *Mould small pears or other fruits from papier mâché pulp following the pulp method on page 17. Cut a cocktail stick into short lengths. Dab the ends with PVA medium and insert into the tops of the fruit to form stalks. Leave the fruits to dry. Apply coloured paint, then sponge with gold paint. Cut leaves from gold paper, fold in half then glue to the fruit stalks.*

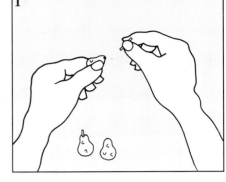

2 *To make the tree, cut a slice 1.5 cm (⅝ in) wide from a kitchen paper towel inner tube. Cover with three layers of papier mâché following the layered method on page 16. Trim the edges level. Attach the ring to the base of a polystyrene cone with strips of newspaper and PVA medium. Cover the cone with pulp following the pulp method on page 17.*

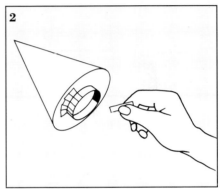

3 *Mould some pears and a partridge from pulp. Press the partridge to the top of the cone tree. Cut a small triangle of thick card for the partridge's beak. Dab the end with PVA medium and press to the bird's head. Set the tree and pears aside for approximately six hours, then attach the pears to the tree with PVA medium.*

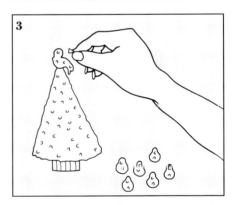

4 *When the model is dry, paint the tree base and the partridge's beak with gold paint. Paint the tree, partridge and pears with Indian inks. Using a sponge, dab gold paint over the entire model. Cut tiny leaves from gold paper and fold in half. Open out the leaves and glue to the pears.*

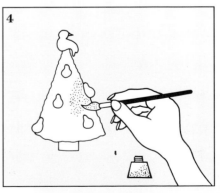

Toy Cupboard

This compendium of practical and amusing games
and toys will entertain your friends, be they
children or adults.

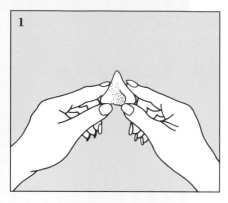

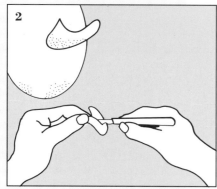

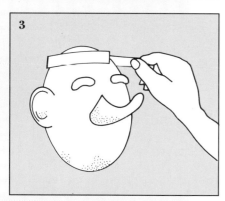

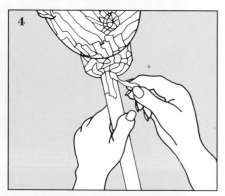

1 *The head of the sailor and pirate is constructed in the same way. Mould an oval of clay for the head 14 cm (5½ in) high for the sailor and 11 cm (4¼ in) for the pirate. Mould a triangle of clay for the nose. Squeeze the corners of the base between thumb and forefinger to form nostrils. Press to the head. Pull the tip of the sailor's nose upwards to form a hook, adding more clay if necessary.*

2 *Roll a sausage of clay for the eyebrows. Bend the ends downwards and cut in half lengthways. Press to the head. Mould a pear shape for the ears, cut in half and flatten each piece. Press to each side of the head. Add detail if you wish by pressing into the ear with a finger.*

3 *For the sailor, roll out a piece of clay 5 mm (¼ in) thick and cut a strip 2 cm (¾ in) wide. Wrap around the head at the top. Roll a large ball of clay, flatten with a rolling pin and press over the top of the head to form a beret. Roll a small ball for the mouth, cut in half and press to the head under the nose. Indent the centre with a pencil. Coil a strip of clay under the head and overlap at the front to make a scarf.*

4 *Cut two corrugated card circles 10.5 cm (4 in) in diameter. In the centres of these circles cut a hole 5.5 cm (2⅛ in) wide and glue the two circles together. Apply five layers of papier mâché to all model pieces following the layered method on page 16. Slice the head in half lengthways through the nose to remove the mould and rejoin following the cut and rejoin method on page 18. Cut a hole under the scarf and insert a wooden stick or length of dowelling. Apply four further layers of papier mâché to the scarf extending the strips onto the stick.*

▼ *This amusing hoop-la toy is reminiscent of traditional English 'end of the pier' games. Simply hold the stick and try to catch the lifebuoy on the sailor's hooked nose. His colourful sea-faring mate, a jaunty pirate glove puppet, is sure to entertain your family and friends. Adapt the techniques required to create other engaging characters.*

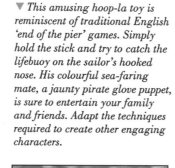

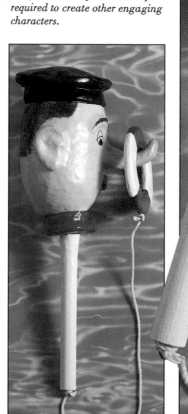

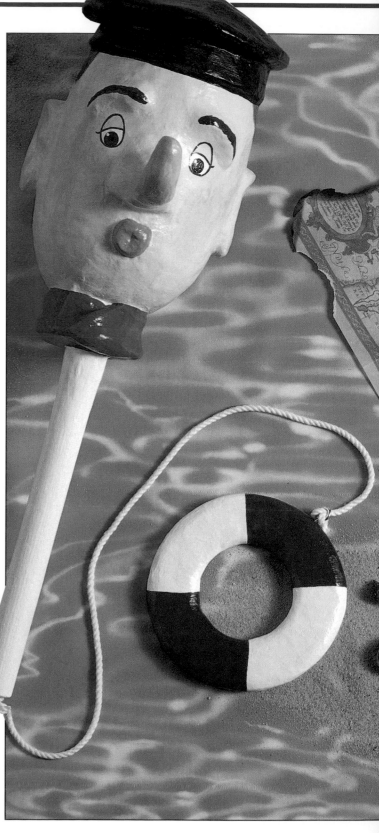

5 *For the pirate, cut a tricorne hat from thick paper using the template on page 114. Cut out the hole and curve the sides upwards between thumb and forefinger. Mould a moustache from clay. Roll out a piece of clay and cut an eyepatch. Press to the head.*

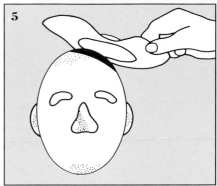

6 *Roll out clay 7 mm (⁵⁄₁₆ in) thick. Cut out a hand using the template on page 115. Pat the cut edges to curve them, then bend the fingers over. Roll two sausages of clay. Press one to the base of the hand and bend the other into a ring large enough to encircle two fingers. Press the ring to the bottom of the head. Smear the moulds with petroleum jelly. Use the template on page 115 to cut two hooks from corrugated card and glue together. Apply five layers of papier mâché to all pieces. Slice the head and hand in half lengthways to remove the moulds and rejoin using PVA medium. Apply four more papier mâché layers to the head and hand.*

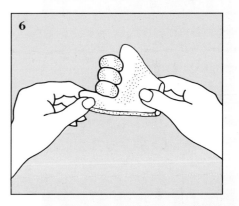

7 *Sand, undercoat and then paint the models (see page 19). For the sailor, screw a screw-eye into the lifebouy and to the end of the stick. Thread cord through both screw-eyes and tie at the end.*

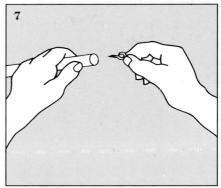

8 *For the pirate, recut the hole under the head. Glue gold braid to the hat rim. Use the template on page 115 to cut two gloves from striped fabric. With right sides facing and taking a 1.5cm (⅝ in) seam allowance, stitch the side seams and shoulder seams, leaving open at the armholes and between the dots at the neck. Turn under 1.5 cm (⅝ in) between the dots and at the armholes. Gather the neck edge around the head hole and the armholes around the hand and hook. Glue the glove securely to the papier mâché pieces. Glue a brass curtain ring to one ear.*

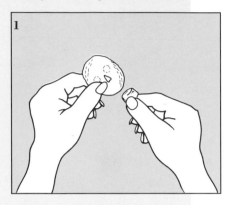

1 *To make a clay mould for the doll's head, roll an oval 4 cm (1½ in) high. Mould a small triangle for the nose and press to the centre of the head. Press the head with your little finger on either side of the nose to form eye sockets. Stroke the base of the head outwards to form a chin. Roll a thick sausage of clay to form the neck. Cut a slice and press under the head.*

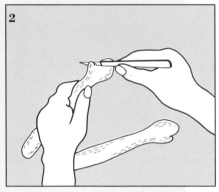

2 *Roll out a large lump of clay to a thickness of 1.5 cm (⅝ in). Use the template on page 115 to cut a body from the clay. Press the neck and head to the top of the body, blending the join with a finger. Pat the cut edges of the body to curve them. To make the arms, roll two sausages approximately 1 cm (⅜ in) thick and 9.5 cm (3¾ in) long. Pat the ends to curve them. Flatten one end of each arm to form hands. Indent a thumb.*

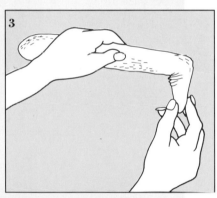

3 *Squeeze the middle of each arm to make elbows, then bend the arms slightly foward. To make the legs, roll two sausages of clay 1.8 cm (⁷⁄₁₀ in) thick and 14.5 cm (5¾ in) long. Pat the ends to curve them and mould the top to fit neatly against the leg edges of the body. Bend the ends of the legs forward at the bottom to form feet. Slightly flatten the feet.*

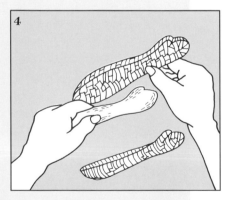

4 *To add definition, squeeze the legs above the feet to make ankles and at the centre to form knees. Smear all pieces with petroleum jelly, then apply five layers of papier mâché following the layered method on page 16. Slice the pieces in half to remove moulds and rejoin following the cut and rejoin method on page 18. Sand and undercoat the doll sections (see page 19).*

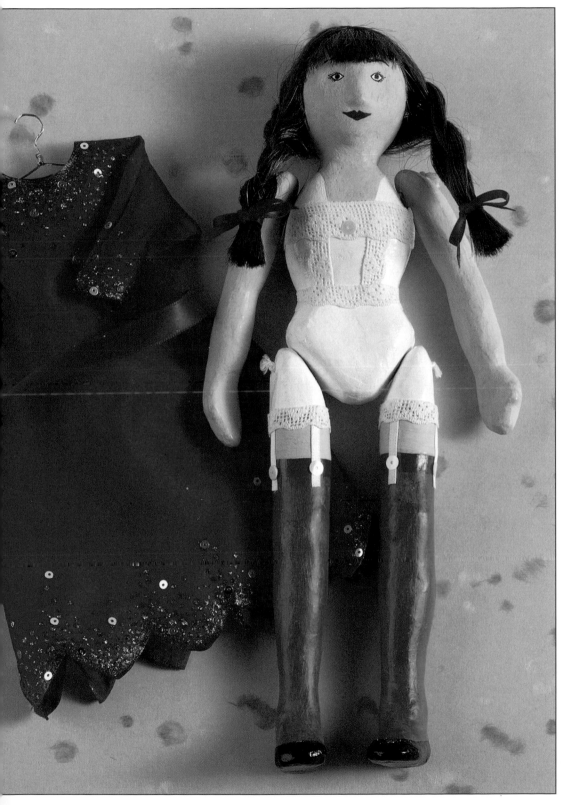

5 *Paint the doll sections – add shoes, stockings and a chemise. Paint the face and rouge the cheeks. Glue on fine ribbon suspenders, lace edging and tiny sequins as buttons. Position the arms and legs against the body, then carefully pierce holes through the top of the arms and body with a thick needle. Thread with embroidery silk, knotting the ends securely on the arms. Join the legs to the body in the same way.*

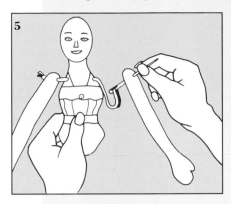

6 *Glue synthetic doll's hair across the forehead as a fringe. Lay 24 cm (9½ in) lengths of doll's hair on tissue paper. Carefully stitch across the centre to form a 'parting'. Tear away the tissue paper. Place the hair on the head with the parting along the centre and glue in position. Tie ribbon in a bow around the hair.*

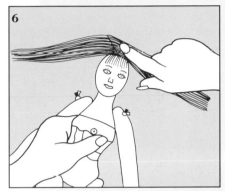

7 *To make the dress, use the template on page 115 to draw one dress front and a pair of dress backs on silky fabric placing the arrow parallel to the selvedge of the fabric. Use a glitter pen to run a line of glitter along the neck and scalloped edges. Add dots of glitter to create a border, positioning sequins on the glitter before it dries. Decorate the shoes with the glitter pen and tiny sequins.*

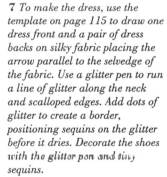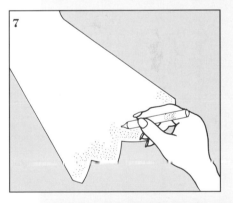

8 *Cut out the dress. Taking a 6 mm (¼ in) seam allowance, stitch the front to the backs along the shoulder and side seams. Stitch the back seam downwards from the dot. Overlap the neck edges and fasten with press-studs. Slip the dress onto the doll and tie a length of ribbon around the waist.*

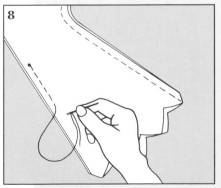

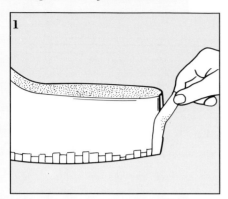

1 *Use the templates on pages 116-117 to cut a base from thick card and a boat, cabin and support from thin card. Stick the lower edge of the boat to the base with brown paper tape following the card mould method on page 14. Glue the overlapped edges together at the stern. Stick the bow slit together edge to edge with brown paper tape.*

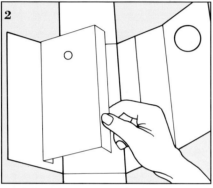

2 *Cut out the handle holes and the porthole on the cabin and support. Score the right side along the broken lines and bend backwards along the scored lines. Mark the support lines on the cabin. Glue the support tabs inside the cabin with the hole at the top and matching the support lines. Fold the cabin into a box shape and stick the edges together with brown paper tape.*

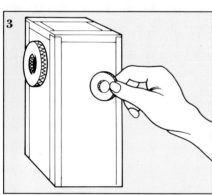

3 *For the front porthole, cut a circle 4.5 cm (1¾ in) in diameter from corrugated card. Cut a hole 3 cm (1¼ in) in diameter in the centre. Glue to the cabin front, matching holes. For the side and back portholes, cut three circles 3.5 cm (1½ in) in diameter from corrugated card. Cut a hole 2 cm (¾ in) in diameter in the centre of each circle. Glue to the sides and back of the cabin, positioning the handle hole at the back in the centre of the back porthole.*

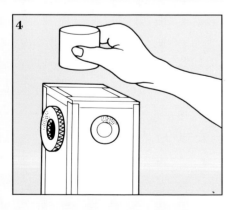

4 *Use the template on page 116 to cut a fish from corrugated card. Cut a section 4 cm (1½ in) wide from a toilet roll tube. Glue to the roof as a funnel. For the lifebouys, cut two circles of corrugated card 4.5 cm (1¾ in) in diameter. Apply three layers of papier mâché to the inside of the boat and to the cabin, lifebouys and fish following the layered method on page 16. When dry, paint the fish on either side.*

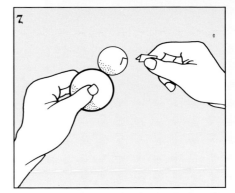

7 To make the seagulls, take three cotton pulp balls 2.5 cm (1 in) in diameter and glue a cotton pulp ball 2 cm (¾ in) in diameter to each to form heads and bodies. Refer to the templates on page 116 to cut three beaks, three tails, two slit wings and four flat wings from thin card. Score beaks and tails along broken lines and fold into a 'V' shape. Use a craft knife to cut 'V'-shaped slits in the seagull heads for the beaks and at the ends of the bodies for the tails. Insert the wide ends of each piece into the slits.

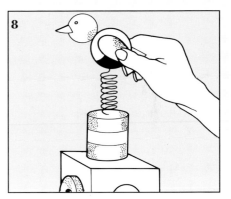

8 Cut slits in each side of one seagull. Insert the slit wings into the slits and bend the wings upwards. Glue flat wings to the remaining birds. Fix the seagulls onto cocktail sticks and paint them. Glue the seagull with the slit wings to the top of the flag pole. Uncoil the spring from a spiral-bound notepad and trim to 6 cm (2½ in) in length with wire cutters. Screw one end into the underside of a seagull.

▲ *Land ahoy! Here is an amusing model for landlubbers. Push the handle in and out of the porthole to make a startled seagull fly out of the cabin.*

5 Trim the papier mâché level on the upper edge of the boat and around the handle hole. Apply five layers of papier mâché to the outside of the boat. Leave to dry, then trim the upper edge level. Sand, fill and undercoat all pieces (see page 19). Paint the pieces with craft paints, retaining the dots marked on the boat.

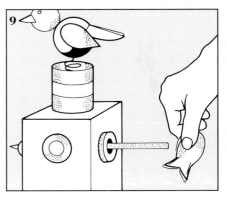

9 Pierce a hole in the centre of the cabin roof inside the funnel and screw the other end of the spiral into the hole. Make a hole in the remaining seagull under the tail. Dab glue onto one end of the rod and insert into the hole. Insert the rod through the front porthole and then the handle holes. Glue the fish to the free end.

6 Using wood dye, stain a 26 cm (10 in) length of wood dowelling 1 cm (⅜ in) thick for the flag pole. Stain an 11 cm (4¼ in) length of 5 mm (¼ in) thick wood dowelling for the seagull rod. For the flag, cut a rectangle of thick paper 10.5 x 4.5 cm (4⅛ x 1¾ in). Glue one end around the top of the flag pole, curving the flag between thumb and forefinger so that it appears to be billowing in the wind. Apply eight layers of papier mâché to the flag, then trim the edges level. Paint the flag.

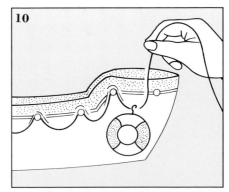

10 Make holes at the dots on the boat and fix a brass paper fastener through each hole. Screw a screw-eye into each lifebouy and thread onto white cord. Drape the cord in loops over each paper fastener with the lifebouys suspended each side of the boat's bow. Tie the cord ends together. Glue the cabin and flag pole to the inside of the boat.

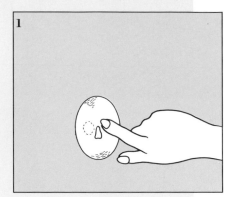

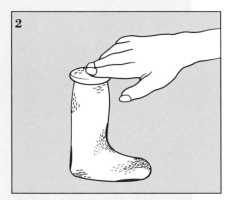

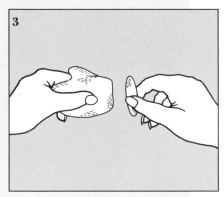

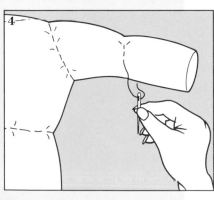

1 *Roll out an oval of clay 6 cm (2½ in) long for the head. Mould a small triangle for the nose and press on the head. Press each side of the nose with a finger to form eye sockets. Build up the chin a little with more clay. Mould two feet 5 cm (2 in) long from clay. Roll sausages for the lower legs and press to the top of the feet, blending the clay over the joins. Cut the legs 6 cm (2½ in) high.*

2 *Roll out flat a lump of clay to 7 mm (⁵⁄₁₆ in) thick and cut out two hands using the templates on page 117. Pat the cut edges to curve the hands. Take three balls of clay 2 cm (¾ in) in diameter and roll out flat to form discs 1 cm (⅜ in) thick. Press to the top of the legs and under the head.*

3 *Roll out flat two sausages of clay 2 cm (¾ in) long to 1 cm (⅜ in) thick. Press against the straight edges of the hands. Smear the head and hand moulds with petroleum jelly. Apply five layers of papier mâché to all the moulds following the layered method on page 16. Leave to dry. Using the cut and rejoin method on page 18, slice the papier mâché off the head, hand and leg moulds, remove the clay and rejoin the papier mâché. Apply a further four layers of papier mâché. Undercoat, fill and sand the head, legs and hands and paint them.*

4 *Cut out two fabric bodies using the template on page 117. Taking a 6 mm (¼ in) seam allowance, stitch together, leaving open the hand and leg openings and the neck opening between the dots. Stitch the inner leg seams as far as the cross. Snip the seam allowance around any curves and to the cross. Turn right side out and fill loosely with toy filling. Stitch along the broken lines through both thicknesses. Turn fabric under 6 mm (¼ in) at the leg, hand, and neck openings and sew around with gathering stitches, leaving one end of the thread unsecured.*

5 *Insert the head into the neck opening and the hands and legs into the hand and leg openings. Draw the loose threads to gather the fabric tightly around the rims and secure the thread with a few stitches on the fabric. Dab sparingly with glue. Draw two pairs of marionette outfits onto fabric using the template on page 117. Draw a strip 55 x 6.5 cm (22 x 2½ in) on fabric for the ruff. Using the relief paint method on page 21, apply relief and glitter paint to the scalloped edges of the outfit and paint a scalloped pattern on one long edge of the ruff. Cut out the fabric, cutting around the scalloped pattern on the ruff. Taking a 6 mm (¼ in) seam allowance, stitch together the front and back of the outfit along the centre front and back seams and along the inner leg seam, leaving the seam open above the dot for the back. Turn the right side out.*

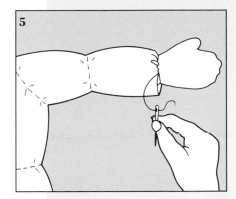

6 *Stitch the front and back together along the shoulder and side seams, leaving neck, arm and leg openings unstitched. Snip through the seam allowance around curves. Gather the inside edge of the ruff to fit the neck. Pin and stitch to the neck. Slip the outfit onto the puppet. Close the opening at the back by turning the fabric under 6 mm (¼ in) and overstitching the seam. Fold a square of fabric 20 x 20 cm (8 x 8 in) diagonally in half. Tie around the head like a turban, tucking the ends under at the front. Glue jewellery stones, sequins shells or feathers to the outfit.*

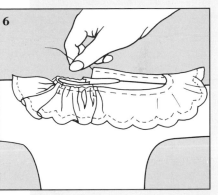

7 *Paint two 20 cm (8 in) lengths of wood batten 2 x 1 cm (¾ x ⅜ in) and drill a hole through the centre of each. Fix together with a cotter pin and washers, available from hardware stores. Fix screw-eyes to the battens in the positions shown on the diagram on page 117. Fix a screw-eye to the back of the neck and pass a length of thread through the eye. Tie each end of the thread to the two head control eyes, as indicated in the diagram. Sew a length of thread to the back of the body at the position indicated by the cross on the body template. Fasten threads to the hands and knees. Tie the back, hand and leg threads to the control screws indicated on the diagram.*

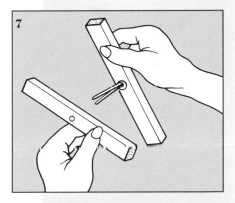

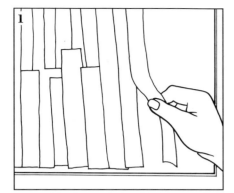

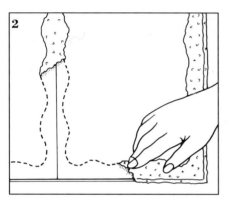

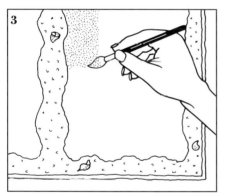

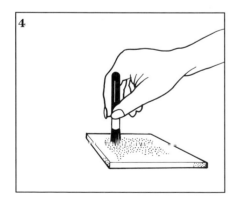

1 *Cut a rectangle of corrugated card 52 x 50.8 cm (20½ x 20 in). Apply four layers of papier mâché to one side following the layered method on page 16. Leave to dry, then apply four layers to the other side. Leave to dry, then sand and fill one side – this will be the upper side of the board.*

2 *Divide the board in half by drawing a line lengthways across the centre. Refer to the template on pages 118-119 and trace the broken lines onto a piece of tracing paper. Centre these lines within each half of the board and transfer onto the surface. Make up some papier mâché pulp following the pulp method on page 17. Dab PVA medium onto the cut edges of the board, onto the border outside the broken lines and onto the central bar between the two halves. Apply the pulp onto these areas, building up to a height of about 6 mm (¼ in).*

3 *Dab some shells with PVA medium and press into the pulp. Leave to dry. Undercoat the board. Use acrylic paints to paint the board blue between the pulp borders. Paint the shells red, orange and apricot. Refer to the template to cut a piece of stencil board using the broken lines as an outline. Transfer the outlines of the yellow shaded areas onto the stencil card with tracing paper and cut out with a craft knife. These will be the apricot and yellow points on the board.*

4 *Place the stencil within the pulp borders on one half of the board and use weights to hold it in position. Apply a thin film of apricot acrylic paint to an old plate or tile. Dab at the paint with a stencil brush.*

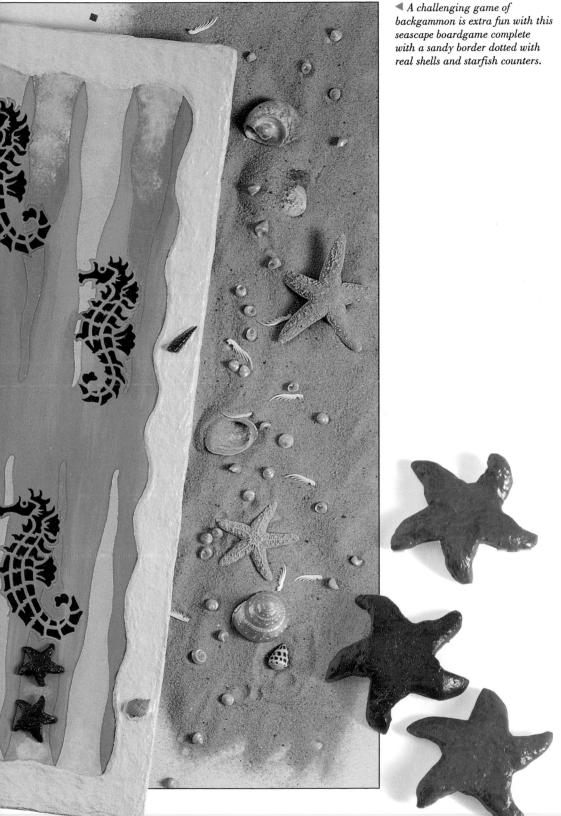

◀ *A challenging game of backgammon is extra fun with this seascape boardgame complete with a sandy border dotted with real shells and starfish counters.*

5 *Apply the paint to alternate cut-outs by holding the brush upright and moving it in a circular motion. Leave to dry then repeat. Stencil the other half of the board in the same way.*

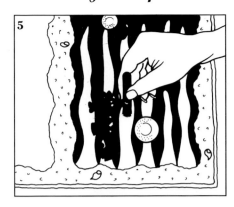

6 *On both halves of the board, stencil the remaining cut-outs with lemon acrylic paint. Then stencil a little lemon paint on all the points. Remove the stencil and transfer the outlines of the red shaded areas onto the stencil card and cut them out. These will be the seahorses. Mask off the point cut-outs close to the seahorse cut-outs with masking tape. Stencil the seahorses on both halves of the board with red acrylic paint.*

7 *Remove the stencil. Paint the pulp border and bar with lemon acrylic paint. Use the template on page 119 to cut a starfish from thin card. Flatten some pulp to approximately 7 mm (⁵⁄₁₆ in) thick and use the template to cut 30 starfishes.*

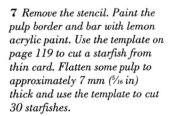

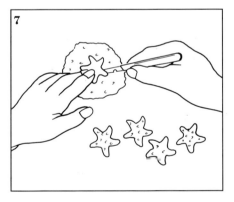

8 *Leave to dry, then paint 15 starfishes in red and the remainder in orange.*

Glittering Prizes

Gold and silver, beads and baubles hold a fascination for many people. This chapter shows how simple models are given vibrancy and designer style with the use of metallic and pearlized paints, glitter and jewellery stones.

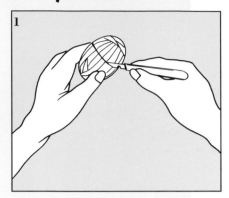

1 *To make the papier mâché eggs, hard boil five eggs for half an hour. Smear one egg with petroleum jelly. This will be the mould for the halved egg. Following the layered method on page 16, apply four layers of papier mâché to the eggs that will remain whole. Apply eight layers to the egg covered with petroleum jelly and leave to dry. Cut this egg in half with a craft knife and remove the mould.*

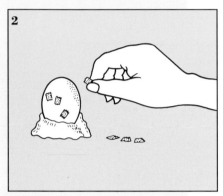

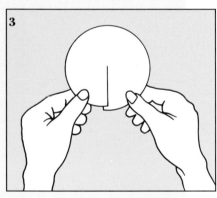

2 *Support the eggs with clay when painting them. Undercoat the eggs and paint with pearlized paint. Paint the inside of the halved egg with gold craft paint. Tear gold paper into small pieces and stick to the eggs using PVA solution. Coat with PVA medium all over. The halved egg can be lined with gold-painted tissue paper, then fastened with fine gold cord.*

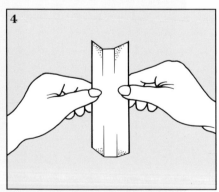

3 *To make the pedestal, take a piece of thin card and cut one circle 13 cm (5 in) in diameter for the dish and one circle 10 cm (4 in) in diameter for the base. Cut a straight line from the rim to the centre of the circle and overlap the straight edges to form shallow cones. Glue in position.*

4 *Use the templates on page 120 to cut one pillar and two wings from thin card. Score the pillar along the broken lines, fold along the broken lines and stick the long edges together with brown paper tape. Glue the pillar upright on the base, then glue the dish on top. Attach a wing to each side of the pillar with strips of newspaper and PVA medium.*

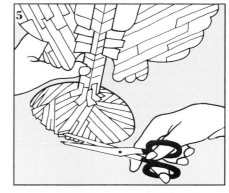

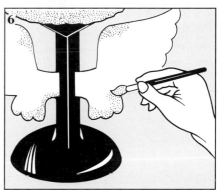

5 *Apply six layers of papier mâché to the model following the layered method on page 16. Tear away the newspaper around the dish circumference to give a deckled edge. Leave to dry. Trim the papier mâché edges around the rim of the base. Fill, sand and undercoat the model.*

6 *Paint the top of the dish and the wings in gold. Paint the rest of the pedestal with pearlized paint.*

◀ *This celestial dish on a pedestal can hold delicate sweets or display beautiful papier mâché eggs.*

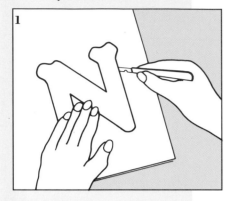

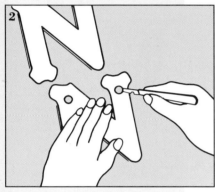

For inspiration, look for attractive lettering in magazines and on posters. Design a letter approximately 16 cm (6½ in) to 23 cm (9 in) high. Draw onto thick card.

1 *Cut out the letter and use it as a template to cut another from thick card.*

2 *If you wish to hang the letter on a wall, cut two holes near the top of one of the letter pieces.*

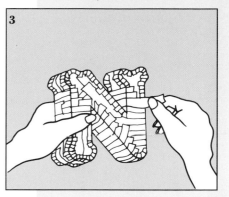

Cut a strip of thin card 5 cm (2 in) to 8 cm (3¼ in) wide. Attach the letters to either side of the strip following the card mould method on page 14. If one letter has hanging holes, place this letter at the back of the model.

3 *Apply five layers of papier mâché following the layered method on page 16. Sand, fill and undercoat the letter (see page 19).*

4 *Spray the letter with metallic spray paints.*

◀ *Create a stunning, graphic display with these giant initials. They can be grouped on a wall or stood upright – on a bookshelf, for instance. Use contrasting lettering styles for added impact.*

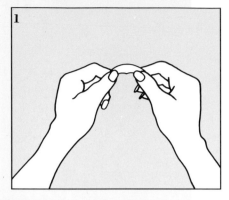

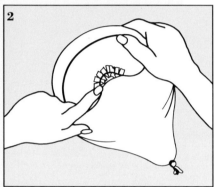

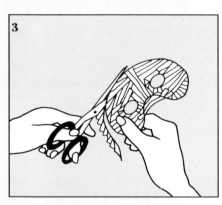

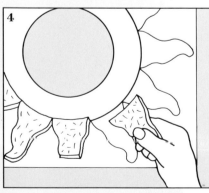

1 *For the moon mask, use the templates on page 120 to cut a mask from paper and a nose from thin card. Pull the nose between a thumb and finger to curve the sides downwards. Blow up a pear-shaped balloon. Gently draw around the mask template on the balloon with a felt pen. The template will not fit the curved balloon exactly so draw the curve for the nose accurately and the rest of the mask roughly.*

2 *Using strips of newspaper and PVA medium, tape the card nose to the balloon along the curves left for the nose in the mask shape, matching the dots. Following the layered method on page 16, apply eight layers of papier mâché to the balloon covering the outlined mask area and the nose. When the papier mâché has dried, remove the mask. Refer to the template to cut out the eye holes.*

3 *Trim the mask edges. Pierce a hole at each side to thread with ribbon. Sand then undercoat the mask. Paint with white craft paint. Use the template on page 120 to draw a moon on the forehead of the mask and paint with silver paint. Cut two lengths of black and silver ribbon. Thread through the holes and knot the ends behind the mask. Fasten the ribbons together in a bow at the side of the mask.*

4 *To make the sun mask, use the template on page 121 to draw the sun on a large sheet of paper. Cut out the two eyes to use as templates later. Cut out an additional single ray and a support ray from paper. Place a dinner plate 21.5 cm (8½ in) in diameter upside down on the centre of the sun. Roll out flat a large piece of clay to 1 cm (⅜ in) thick. Use the single ray template to cut out 11 rays and place them around the plate on the drawing. Use the support ray template to cut out the twelfth ray and place it on the drawing at the bottom of the plate.*

5 *Pat the cut edges of the rays to curve them. Blend the clay onto the plate by stroking the clay towards the plate. Tape the eye templates to the plate – this will help you position the facial features. Roll out flat a lump of clay to 6 mm (¼ in) thick. Mould a pair of lips, indenting a line across the centre.*

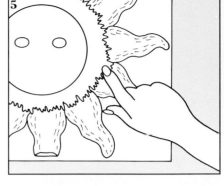

6 *Mould a triangle from clay for the nose. Squeeze the lower corners between thumb and finger to form nostrils. Press the nose and lips to the face. Roll a thin sausage of clay for eyebrows. Bend the ends downwards and press onto the plate above the eyes. Roll two balls of clay 2 cm (¾ in) in diameter. Flatten the balls and press onto the plate under the eyes as cheeks.*

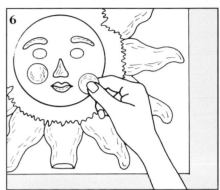

7 *Smear the mould and paper with petroleum jelly. Apply ten layers of papier mâché, following the layered method on page 16 and extending the newspaper onto the greased paper. There is no need to apply papier mâché to the straight end of the support ray. When dry, remove the mould and paper. Trim the papier mâché edges of the rays. Draw the eyes on the mask and cut out with a craft knife.*

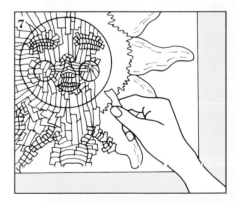

8 *Slip a length of dowelling 2 cm (¾ in) in diameter behind the support ray. Tape securely to the mask with strips of newspaper and PVA medium. Glue a bead to the end of the dowelling. Sand and undercoat the mask. Rub on gold wax gilt (available from art stores or suppliers). Buff to a lustre finish, then varnish the mask.*

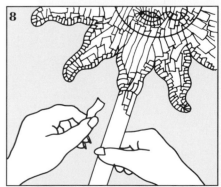

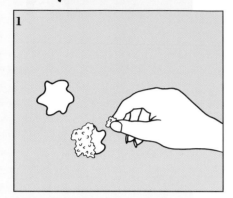

1 To make the cacti, teapot and coffee pot and the flower-shaped earrings, cut the motifs from thin card using the templates on page 120. Spread with PVA medium, then apply papier mâché pulp following the pulp method on page 17. Pierce holes at the top of the cacti, teapot and coffee pot. Leave to dry.

2 Paint the flower earring with craft paint, then coil brass picture hanging wire into a spiral and attach to the flowers with strong glue. Glue clip-on earring fittings to the back. Paint the cacti, teapot and coffee pot with Indian inks. Add details to the teapot and coffee pot with gold Indian ink.

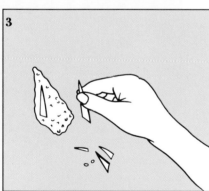

3 The heart stickpin, mirrored earrings and pendant are made by moulding shapes from papier mâché pulp following the pulp method on page 17. Smash a handbag mirror by wrapping it in kitchen paper towels and hitting it with a hammer. Handling the mirror pieces carefully, dab PVA medium onto the back and press into the pulp. Embed jewellery stones in the same way. Pierce a hole in the point of the heart and in the top of the pendant.

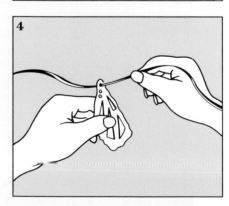

4 Leave to dry. Paint earrings with Indian inks, blending the colours together. Apply glitter paint, then glue clip-on earring fittings to the back. Paint the pendant with pearlized paints and thread onto ribbon. Spread PVA medium on the heart and sprinkle with sequin dust. Leave to dry, then shake off any excess. Fix a drop bead to the point with jump rings and a pendant holder. Glue a stickpin to the back.

5 Use a plastic bottle as a mould for the bangle and smear with petroleum jelly. Apply eight layers of papier mâché following the layered method on page 16, wrapping newspaper strips around the mould. When dry, slip the papier mâché off the mould and trim the edges level. Apply eight more layers around the centre, then add a final layer using giftwrap.

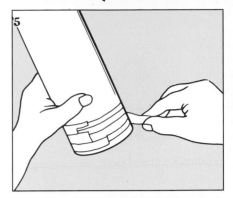

6 To make the star earrings, cut two stars from corrugated card using the template on page 120. Apply three layers of papier mâché following the layered method on page 16. Pierce a hole at the dots. Apply pearlized paint, then dab with gold paint using a sponge. Glue a jewellery stone to the centre. Fix a drop bead to the centre bottom of each earring with jump rings threaded through the hole and a pendant holder which, in turn, is threaded through the bead.

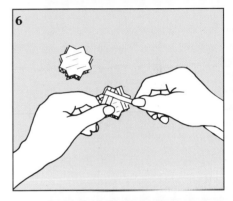

7 For the necklace, roll papier mâché pulp balls following the pulp method on page 17. Using a thick needle, pierce a hole through each bead and leave to dry. Push beads onto cocktail sticks to paint them. Using a sponge, dab with glossy paint in two different colours. Thread the beads onto a length of strong thead. Fasten each end onto torpedo clasps.

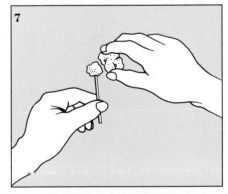

8 To complete the drop earrings, thread a large jump ring or pendant holder through the hole at the top of each earring, then attach to a small jump ring. Affix to earring wires.

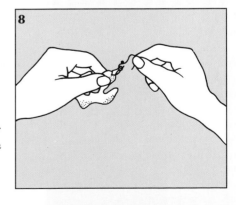

◀ Here is an exciting collection of papier mâché jewellery that is both simple and fun to make. The techniques used can easily be adapted to create a wide range of designer-style accessories.

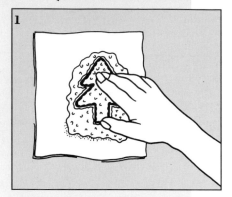

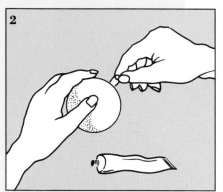

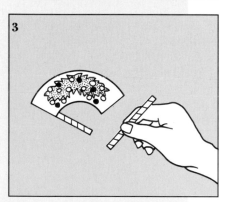

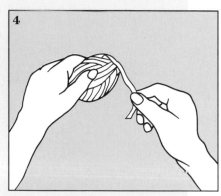

1 *For the Christmas tree decoration, make a quantity of papier mâché pulp following the pulp method on page 17. Roll the pulp out onto an old plastic bag to a thickness of approximately 6 mm (¼ in). Press a Christmas pastry cutter into the pulp. Scrape away the pulp around the outside of the cutter. Pierce a hole at the top and attach jewellery stones to the decoration with PVA medium. When dry, apply paint. Add a little glitter paint.*

2 *To make the round bauble, bend a short length of wire into a 'U' shape. Dab glue onto each end and insert into a polystyrene ball. Spread PVA medium onto the ball. Scrunch pieces of soft, coloured paper and press onto the ball. Leave to dry, then dab with silver and glitter paint at random.*

3 *Use the template on page 123 to cut a fan from thin card. Cut two strips of card 8 cm x 5 mm (3¼ x ¼ in). Cover the fan and card strips with torn strips of giftwrap following the layered method on page 16. Cut a motif from giftwrap and attach to the fan with PVA medium. Glue the card strips along the straight edges of the fan – one to the top of the fan and one to the underside. Fasten the overlapped ends of the strips together with thread and small tassels.*

4 *To make the egg, apply torn strips of tissue paper to a polystyrene egg following the layered method on page 16. Bend a short length of wire into a 'U' shape. Dab glue onto each end and insert into the top of the egg. Bend soft wire, bonsai wire for example, which is available from garden centres or suppliers, into a spiralled 'S' shape and glue onto the egg.*

5 *To make the mauve ring, select a large curtain ring and bind with narrow strips of mauve tissue paper. Glue in place with PVA medium. Dab PVA medium onto the covered ring and sprinkle with sequin dust. Leave to dry, then shake off the excess. Glue plastic flowers to the top of the ring.*

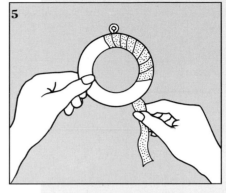

6 *For the basket, glue one end of a strip of thin card to each side of a bottle cap to form a handle. Apply papier mâché pulp to the cap following the pulp method on page 17. Leave to dry. Paint the basket, then glue a piece of dried-flower-arranging foam inside the basket. Mount dried flowers and small fir cones onto wires and insert into the foam. Fasten a ribbon bow around the handle.*

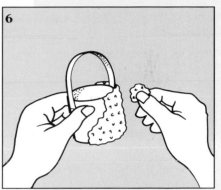

7 *To make the urn, use the template on page 123 to cut an urn shape from corrugated card. Apply three layers of papier mâché to the urn on both sides following the layered method on page 16. Paint the urn and decorate with metallic paper shapes applied with glue. Twist two lengths of silver wire together and bend into curved handle shapes. Hold the ends of a handle against each side of the urn and pierce a hole level with the decoration at each end. Dab glue onto the wire ends and insert into the holes.*

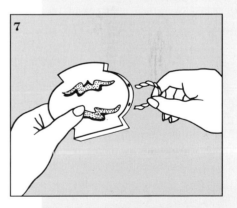

8 *For the tassel, wrap the hanging threads of a large tassel with baking (aluminum) foil for protection. Apply two layers of papier mâché to the tassel knot following the layered method on page 16. Apply a final layer using strips of patterned giftwrap. Leave to dry. Trim the lower edge of the papier mâché level. Highlight the pattern on the giftwrap with glitter paint. Remove the foil. Attach lengths of thread to the top of the tassel, fan and urn using a thick needle. Tie lengths of thread through the hole of the Christmas tree and around the wire of the bauble and egg. Tie thread round the ring and the handle of the basket.*

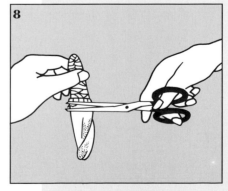

Artful Antiquities

Time and again, it is the riches of the past that inspire contemporary crafts. Look to history for an endless supply of ideas that can be adapted for today's lifestyle or simply recreate a time-honoured classic design.

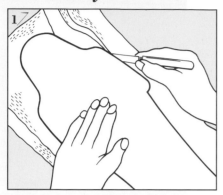

1 *Roll out a lump of clay to a thickness of 3 cm (1¼ in). Use the template on page 122 to cut out a mummy with a dinner knife. Pat the top cut edge with a finger to curve it, then turn the mummy over. Roll out another piece of clay to a thickness of 6 mm (¼ in) and cut out upper body, wig, face and sarcophagus pieces using the templates on page 122.*

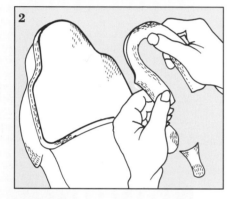

2 *Pat the edges of the face, sarcophagus, inner edge of the wig and lower edge of the upper body with a finger to curve them. Place the upper body onto the mummy. Place the other pieces in position.*

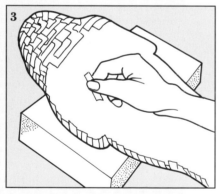

3 *Pat the outer edges of the mummy to curve them. Mould a tiny triangle of clay for the nose and press onto the face. Press the face on each side of the nose with a little finger to form eye sockets. Smear petroleum over the entire mummy. Apply a layer of papier mâché to the top of the model following the layered method on page 16. Turn the mummy over and continue applying the layers on the underside, balancing the mummy on a small box to avoid squashing the face.*

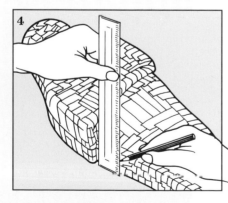

4 *Continue building up layers of papier mâché in the same way until ten have been applied. Sand and fill the mummy (see page 19). Draw a line along the side of the mummy 2 cm (¾ in) above the base. Cut along the line with a craft knife and remove the clay. Cut a strip of thin card 70 x 2 cm (27½ x ¾ in).*

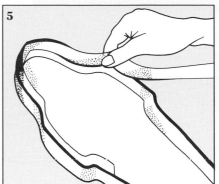

5 *Glue the strip inside the rim of the lower section extending it 1 cm (⅜ in) above the cut edge.*

6 *Apply three layers of papier mâché inside the lower section. When dry, trim the papier mâché level with the card strip. Undercoat, then paint the mummy with gold craft paint inside and out. Paint the wig sarcophagus and eyes with black craft paint. Emphasize the eyes with lemon-coloured paint and highlight the nose and mouth with copper craft paint. Add decorative details in gold and copper paint.*

◀ *Capture the mystique of ancient Egypt with a regal mummy box. Paint the box simply in sumptuous gold or embellish it with rich patterns and hieroglyphics.*

Artful Antiquities

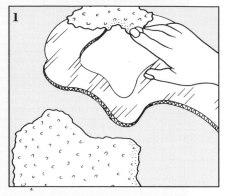

1 Use corrugated card to cut three hand mirrors using the template on page 122. To make the mirror front, cut along the 'front' cutting line on one mirror piece. Cut along the 'middle' cutting line on a second piece to form the mirror middle. The remaining piece will form the mirror back. Make a quantity of papier mâché pulp following the pulp method on page 17. Spread PVA medium over the top and cut-out edges of the mirror front and over the underside of the mirror back. Apply pulp to the mirror front and back on top of the PVA medium.

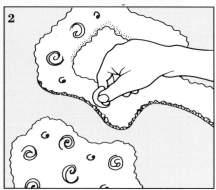

2 Leave to dry for a few hours, then stamp a shell into the pulp to create an embossed design. Experiment with the design on clay beforehand. If you are not satisfied with the design on the pulp, smooth it away with a finger and start again. Leave to dry. Undercoat the mirror front on the inside edges of the cut-out area.

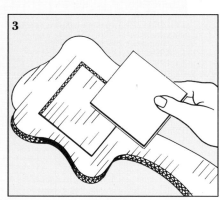

3 Paint the edges with craft paint – this is easier to paint before the mirror is assembled. Glue the mirror middle and back together. Glue a square mirror tile 10 x 10 cm (4 x 4 in) within the middle cut-out area. If the corrugated card is thicker than the mirror, glue squares of thick paper 10 x 10 cm (4 x 4 in) behind the mirror until its surface is level with the surrounding card. Glue the mirror front on top.

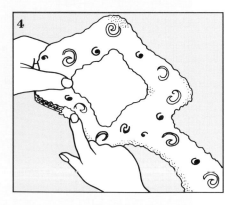

4 Spread pulp over the corrugated card edges along the sides of the hand mirror. Leave to dry, then continue to undercoat the entire mirror. Apply paint – blue and aquamarine craft paints were used for the mirror pictured here and the colours blended together with a paintbrush. Leave to dry, then dab with gold paint from a sponge.

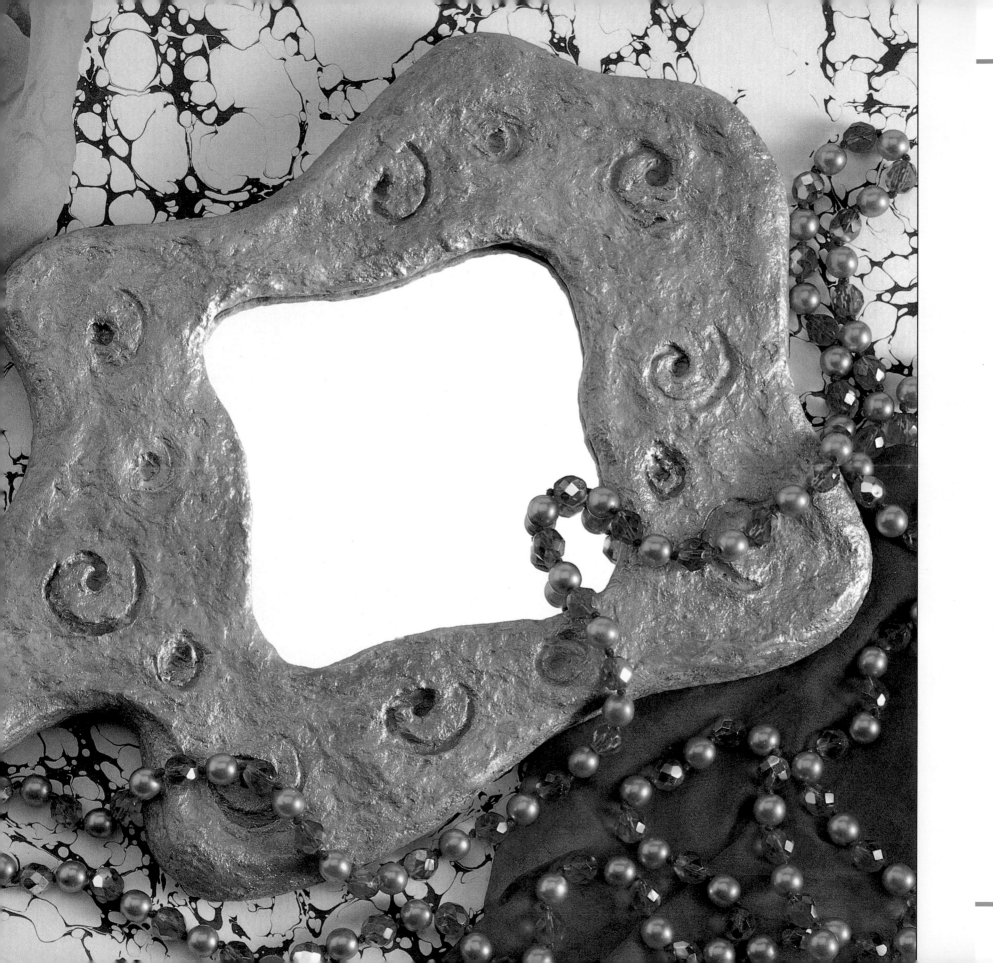

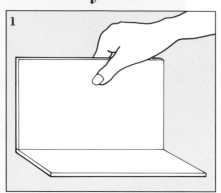

1 *To make the letter rack, use four-sheet thickness mounting board to cut rectangles 24 x 16.5 cm (9½ x 6½ in) for the back, 24 x 8 cm (9½ x 3¼ in) for the front and 24 x 6 cm (9½ x 2⅜ in) for the base. Refer to the diagram on page 123 to cut two side panels. Glue the back upright onto one long edge of the base, holding it in position while the glue dries.*

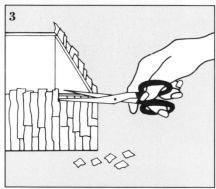

2 *Glue the side panels upright onto the base, matching the short edges with the base and the long edges with the back. Glue the front upright onto the remaining long edge of the base and to the short edges of the side panels.*

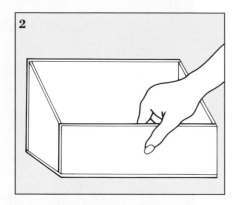

3 *Apply five layers of papier mâché to the outside of the letter rack following the layered method on page 16. Extend the ends of the newspaper strips above the edges of the board. For the pencil-box lid, apply five layers of papier mâché in the same way to the lid of a purchased pencil box. When dry, trim the upper edges of the letter rack level with the mounting board. Trim the papier mâché level with the edges of the pencil-box lid.*

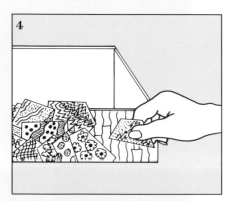

4 *Cut scraps of giftwrap and magazine pictures into uneven shapes. Apply the shapes as a final layer to the papier mâché, trimming the edges when dry. Using acrylic paint in a co-ordinating colour, paint the base of the pencil box and the inside of the letter rack and pencil-box lid. Varnish the letter rack and the pencil box inside and out with PVA medium.*

◀ *Crazy patchwork is a nineteenth-century needlecraft in which fabric patches are arranged in a random pattern. This practical letter rack and pencil box are covered with patterned paper to achieve the same effect.*

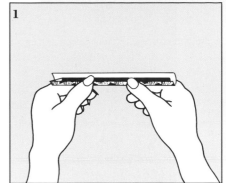

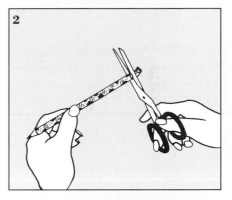

To cover a pencil, cut a strip of giftwrap as long as the pencil and wide enough to wrap around it.

1 Spray the back of the strip with spray adhesive, then wrap it around the pencil. Hold the strip in place while the glue dries.

2 Trim away any excess paper at the ends of the pencil with a pair of scissors.

◀ *This handsome tea tray is adorned with découpage. Intricately cut paper motifs are arranged and glued in attractive designs then sealed with coats of varnish. Découpage was a highly popular form of decoration in the Victorian era.*

Smear the top of a tin or plastic tea tray with petroleum jelly. Apply layers of papier mâché on top until the papier mâché measures 6 mm (¼ in) thick following the layered method on page 16. Trim the papier mâché level with the edge of the tray. Remove the tray. Sand, fill and undercoat the tray (see page 19).

1 Paint the tray all over with black craft paint. Cut out motifs from giftwrap and arrange on the tray.

2 Spray the back of the motifs with spray adhesive and place in position. Varnish the tray all over with six coats of polyurethane gloss varnish.

103

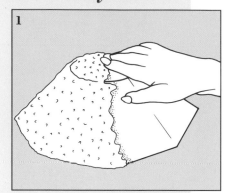

1 *Select a large bowl and a smaller bowl as moulds for the bowl and base respectively. Turn the large bowl upside down and smear with petroleum jelly. Apply papier mâché pulp to the outside surface following the pulp method on page 17. Dab PVA medium around the rim and press a row of shells into the pulp. Leave to dry.*

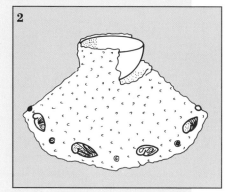

2 *Remove the mould. Smear the outside of the small bowl with petroleum jelly and place it upturned onto the pulp bowl, base to base. Apply pulp to the small bowl blending it onto the pulp bowl.*

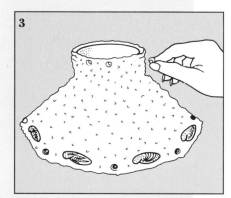

3 *Dab PVA medium around the rim and press a row of tiny shells into the pulp and leave to dry. Remove the mould and undercoat the entire bowl. Dab co-ordinating coloured craft paints onto the bowl and blend the colours together with a paintbrush. Dark orange, orange and yellow paints were used on this bowl.*

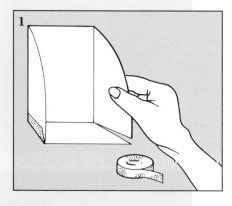

1 *To make the candle sconce, refer to the templates on page 123 to cut a candle sconce and candle holder from thin card. Score along the broken lines. Bend backwards along the scored lines. Stick the edges of the base and the lower edge of the sides together with brown paper tape. Stick the ends of the candle holder together edge to edge with brown paper tape.*

2 *Cut two squares of corrugated card 3.5 x 3.5 cm (1½ x 1½ in). Glue together. Centre the card on top of the candle holder and glue together. Saw an 8.5 cm (3½ in) length of 2 cm (¾ in) thick balsa wood dowelling for the candle. Apply five layers of papier mâché to the sconce, candle holder and candle following the layered method on page 16. Leave to dry, then trim level the base of the candle holder and the candle.*

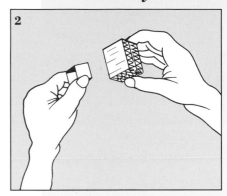

3 *Glue the candle holder to the centre of the sconce base. To form the candle 'drips', make a little papier mâché pulp following the pulp method on page 17. Roll the pulp into suitable shapes and glue to the candle with PVA medium. Using a thick needle, make a hole in the candle top for the wick. Undercoat the sconce and candle. Paint the sconce with silver craft paint.*

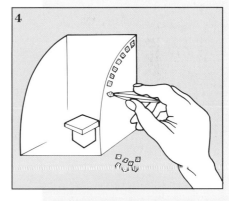

4 *Cut squares 5 x 5 mm (¼ x ¼ in) from glossy magazine pages. Arrange in a design on one side of the sconce, cutting the squares to fit together. Either copy the scorpion motif or apply a border of squares only for simplicity. Use a pair of tweezers to position and glue the pieces in place. Apply a mosaic design to the other side of the sconce. Add a border of squares to the inner edge of the sconce.*

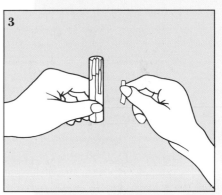

5 *Rub the candle with a soft white wax crayon to give a realistic waxy effect. Varnish the candle with a sealer specifically designed for use on gilded surfaces, available from art stores or suppliers. Coat a length of black stranded cotton embroidery thread with PVA medium. Leave to dry, then glue a short length upright in the candle hole as a wick. Glue the candle centrally onto the candleholder.*

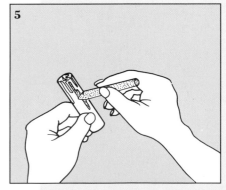

Diagrams and Templates

The following pages present the diagrams and templates for the projects. The diagrams are constructed from measurements. Use a ruler and set square to draw the pieces onto card to use as a template. It is important to follow either the metric or imperial measurement but not a combination of both.

The templates printed in blue are reduced in size. To enlarge, draw a grid of 1.4 cm (⁹⁄₁₆ in) squares. Copy the design square by square using the lines as a guide. Alternatively, enlarge templates on a photocopier to 141% (or A4 enlarged to A3). To make a complete pattern for symmetrical shapes, place the pattern on a piece of folded paper matching the 'place to fold' line to the folded edge. Cut out and open the pattern out flat to use.

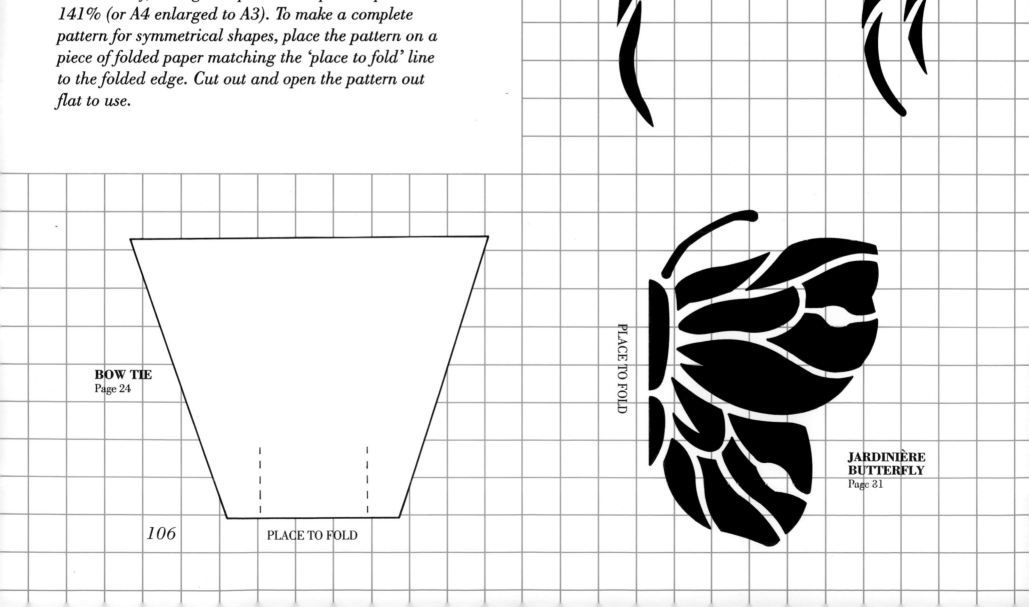

PLACE TO FOLD

JARDINIÈRE SWAG
Page 31

BOW TIE
Page 24

PLACE TO FOLD

JARDINIÈRE BUTTERFLY
Page 31

106   PLACE TO FOLD

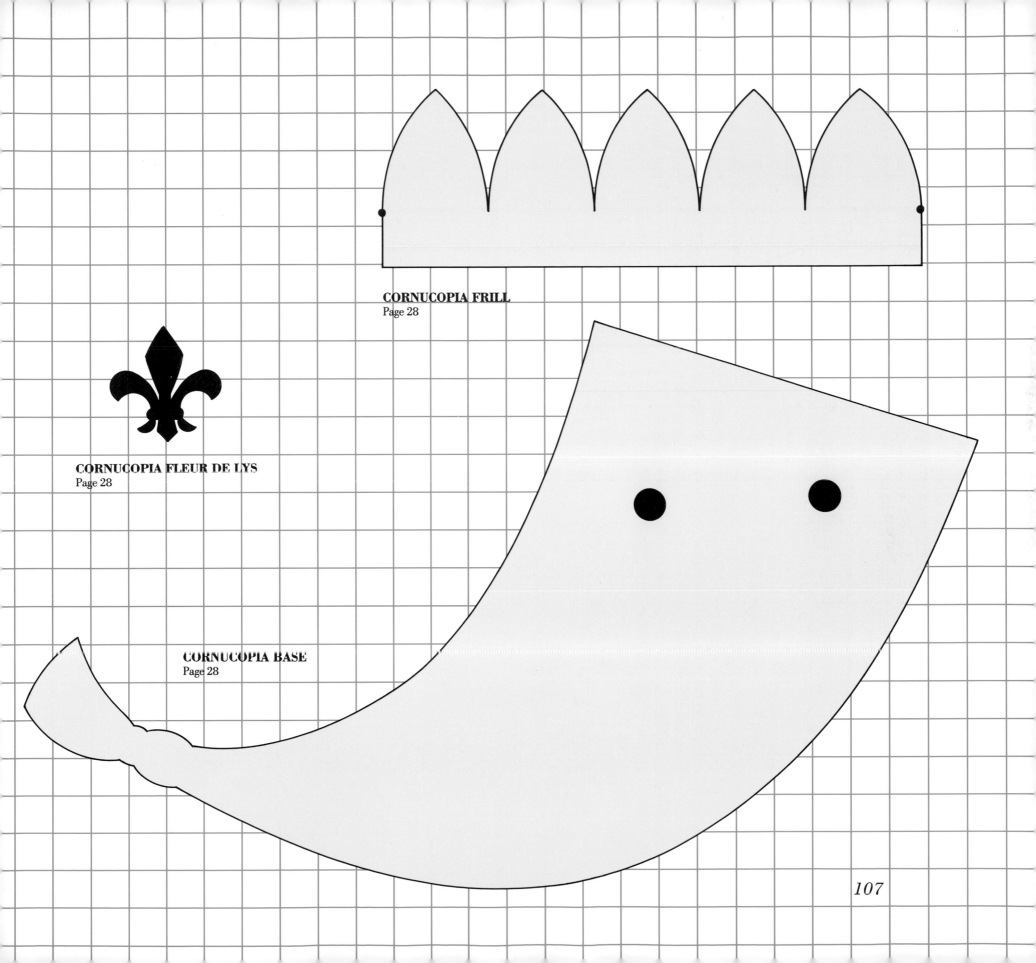

CORNUCOPIA FRILL
Page 28

CORNUCOPIA FLEUR DE LYS
Page 28

CORNUCOPIA BASE
Page 28

107

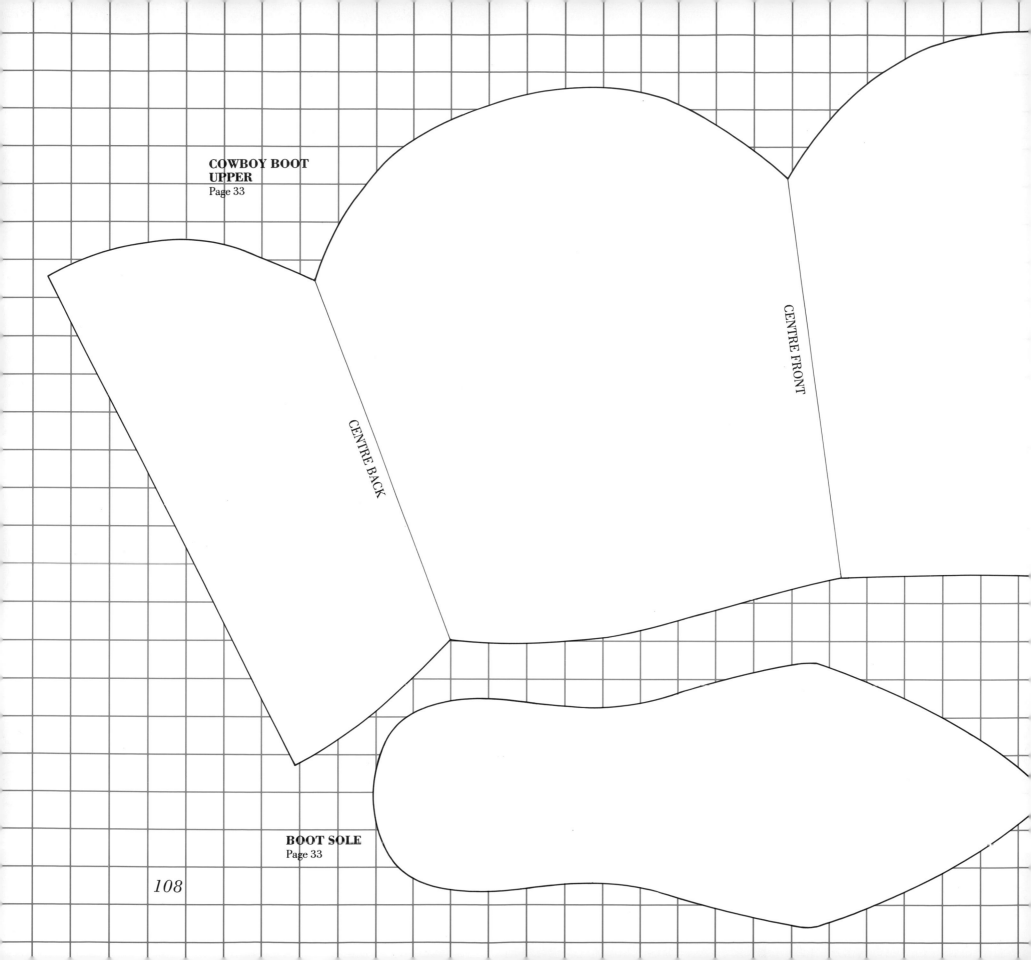

**COWBOY BOOT
UPPER**
Page 33

CENTRE BACK

CENTRE FRONT

BOOT SOLE
Page 33

108

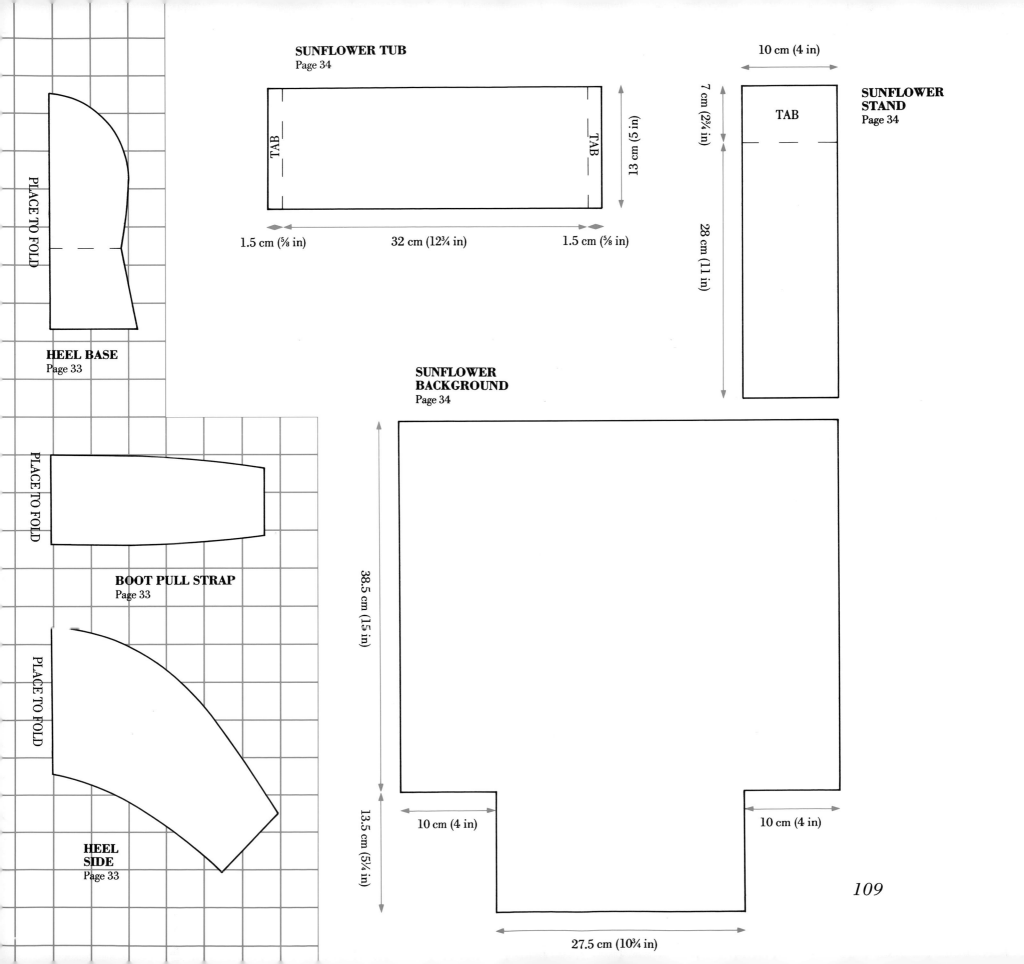

SUNFLOWER TUB
Page 34

TAB

TAB

13 cm (5 in)

1.5 cm (⅝ in)   32 cm (12¾ in)   1.5 cm (⅝ in)

10 cm (4 in)

SUNFLOWER STAND
Page 34

TAB

7 cm (2¾ in)

28 cm (11 in)

PLACE TO FOLD

HEEL BASE
Page 33

PLACE TO FOLD

BOOT PULL STRAP
Page 33

PLACE TO FOLD

HEEL SIDE
Page 33

SUNFLOWER BACKGROUND
Page 34

38.5 cm (15 in)

13.5 cm (5¼ in)

10 cm (4 in)

10 cm (4 in)

27.5 cm (10¾ in)

109

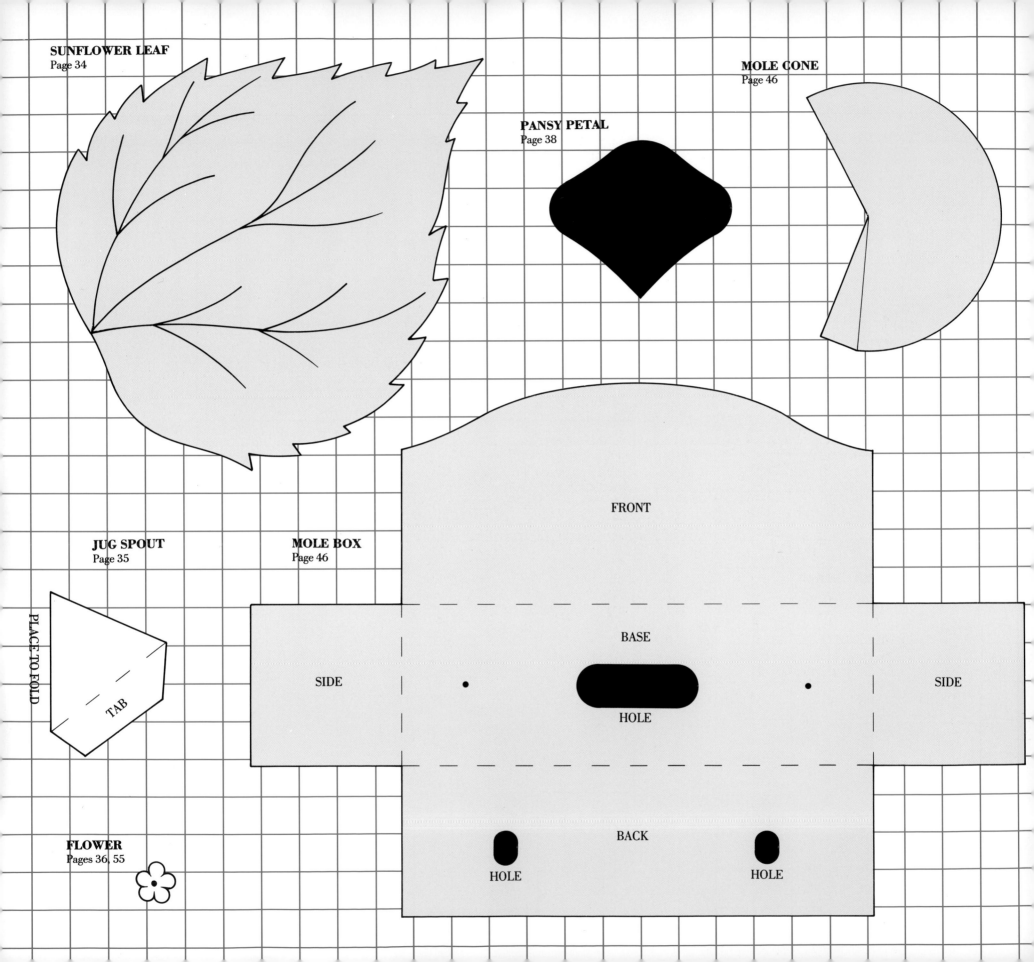

SUNFLOWER LEAF
Page 34

PANSY PETAL
Page 38

MOLE CONE
Page 46

JUG SPOUT
Page 35

MOLE BOX
Page 46

PLACE TO FOLD

TAB

FRONT

BASE

SIDE

SIDE

HOLE

FLOWER
Pages 36, 55

BACK

HOLE

HOLE

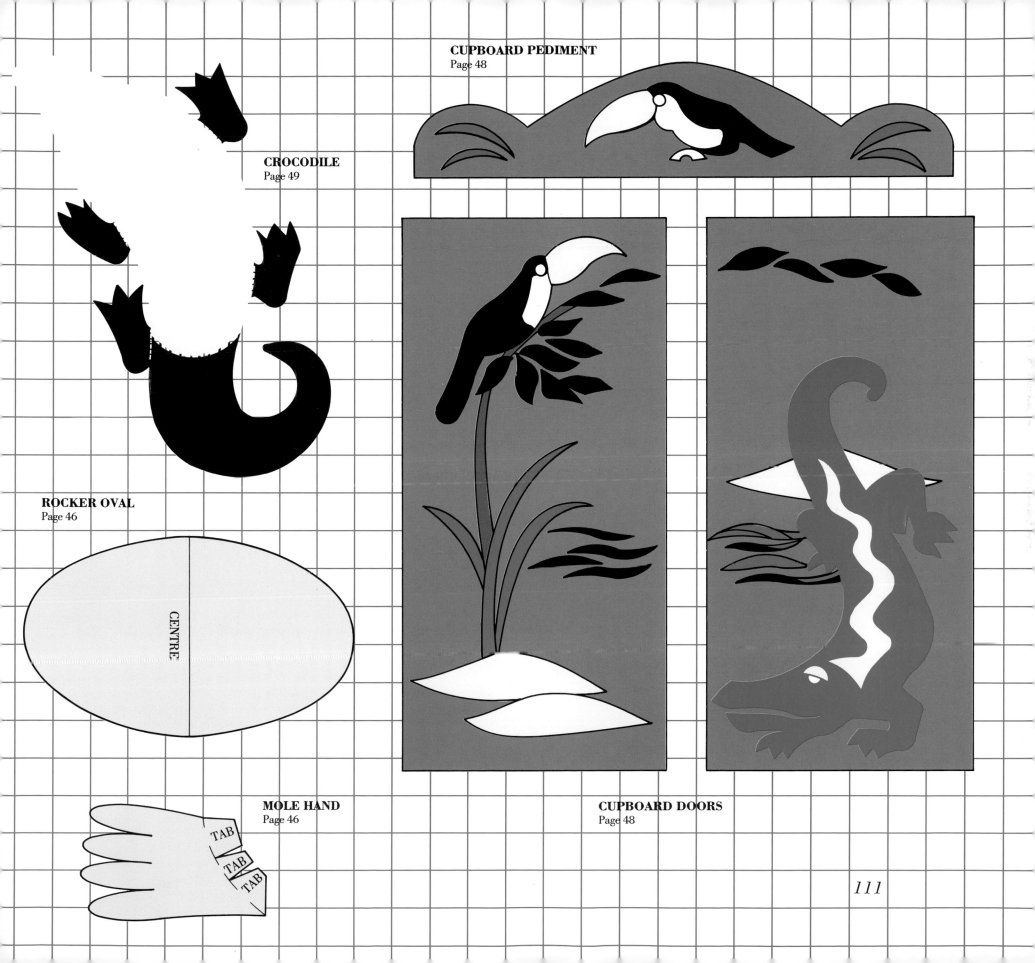

CROCODILE
Page 49

CUPBOARD PEDIMENT
Page 48

ROCKER OVAL
Page 46

CENTRE

MOLE HAND
Page 46

TAB
TAB
TAB

CUPBOARD DOORS
Page 48

111

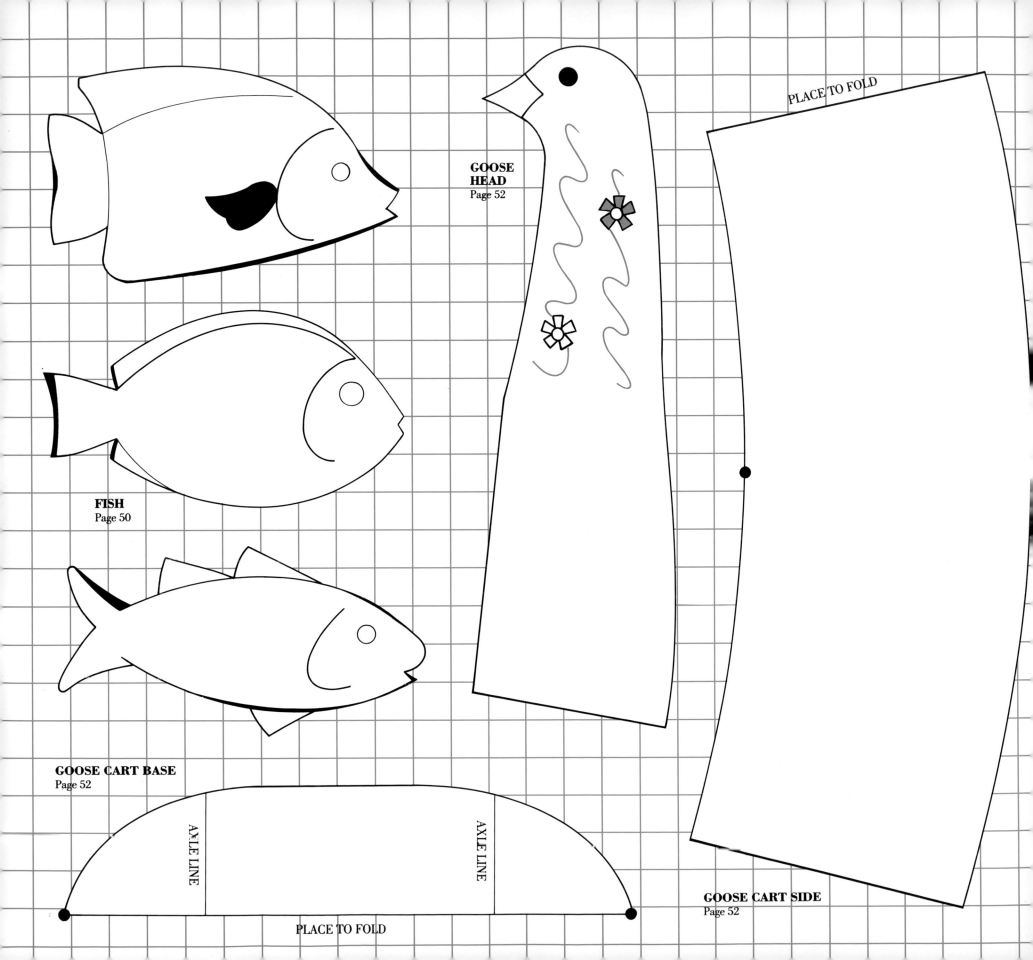

GOOSE
HEAD
Page 52

FISH
Page 50

GOOSE CART BASE
Page 52

AXLE LINE

AXLE LINE

PLACE TO FOLD

PLACE TO FOLD

GOOSE CART SIDE
Page 52

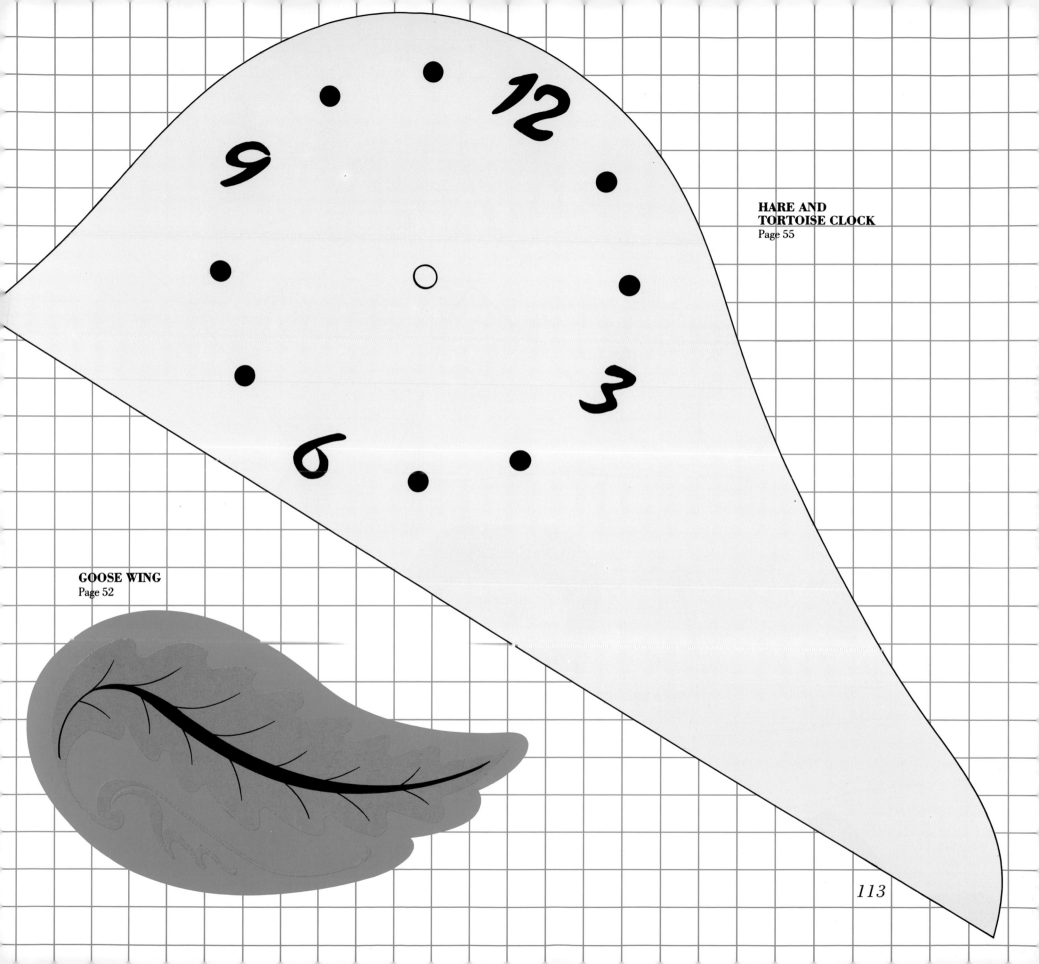

**HARE AND
TORTOISE CLOCK**
Page 55

GOOSE WING
Page 52

113

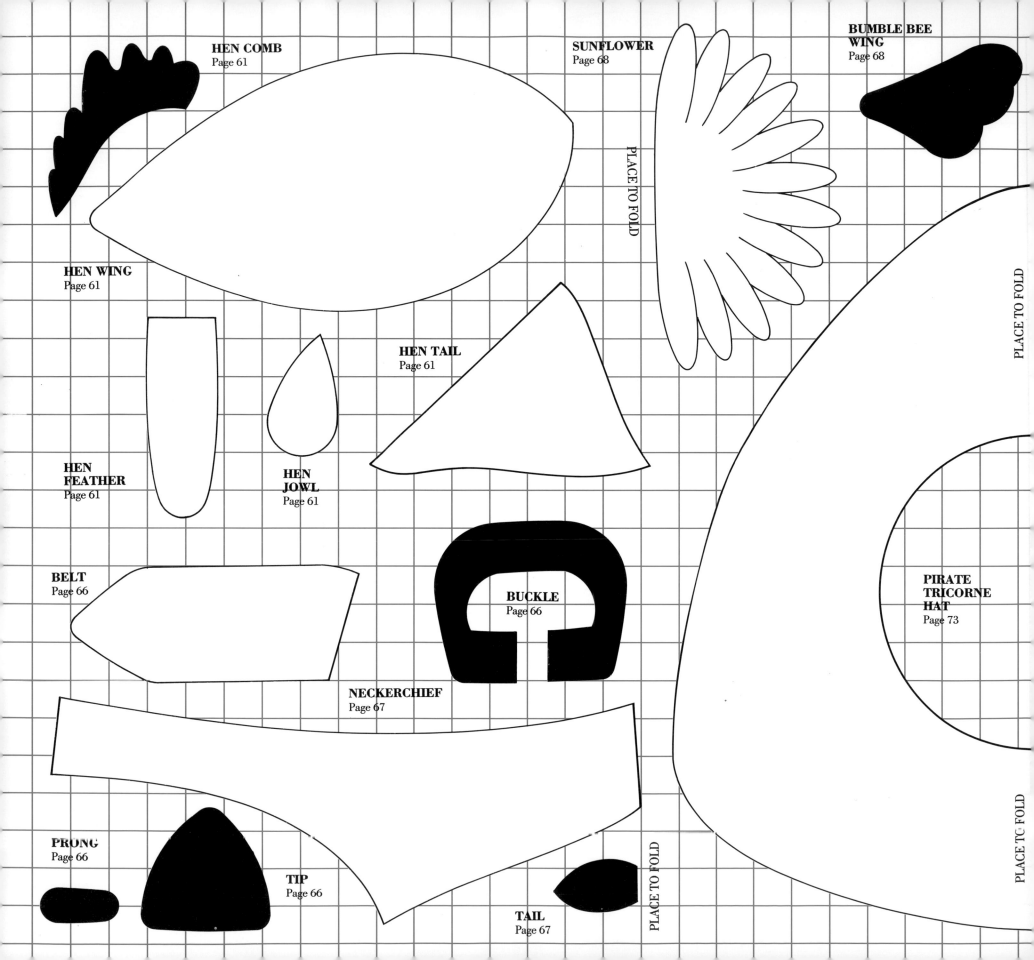

HEN COMB
Page 61

SUNFLOWER
Page 68

BUMBLE BEE WING
Page 68

PLACE TO FOLD

PLACE TO FOLD

HEN WING
Page 61

HEN TAIL
Page 61

HEN FEATHER
Page 61

HEN JOWL
Page 61

BELT
Page 66

BUCKLE
Page 66

PIRATE TRICORNE HAT
Page 73

NECKERCHIEF
Page 67

PRONG
Page 66

TIP
Page 66

TAIL
Page 67

PLACE TO FOLD

PLACE TO FOLD

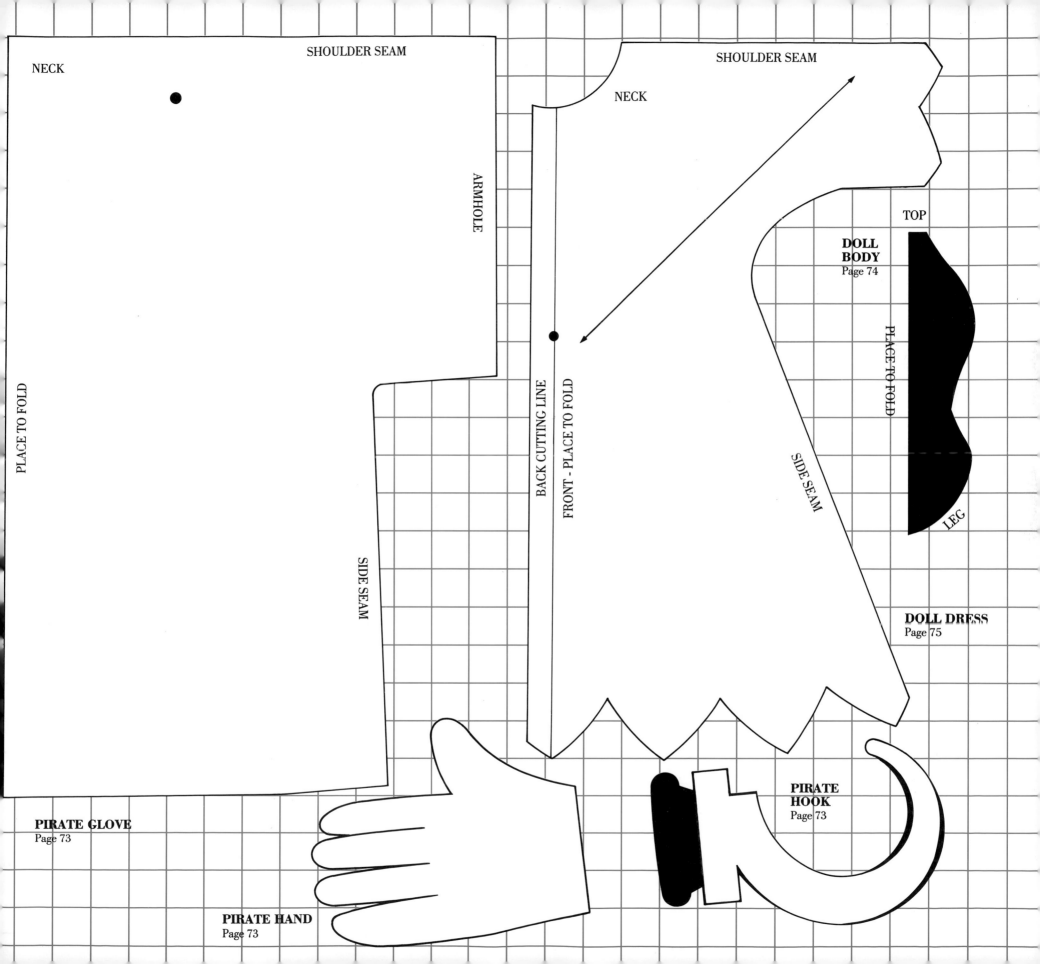

NECK

SHOULDER SEAM

SHOULDER SEAM

NECK

ARMHOLE

PLACE TO FOLD

BACK CUTTING LINE

FRONT - PLACE TO FOLD

SIDE SEAM

SIDE SEAM

TOP

DOLL BODY
Page 74

PLACE TO FOLD

LEG

DOLL DRESS
Page 75

PIRATE GLOVE
Page 73

PIRATE HAND
Page 73

PIRATE HOOK
Page 73

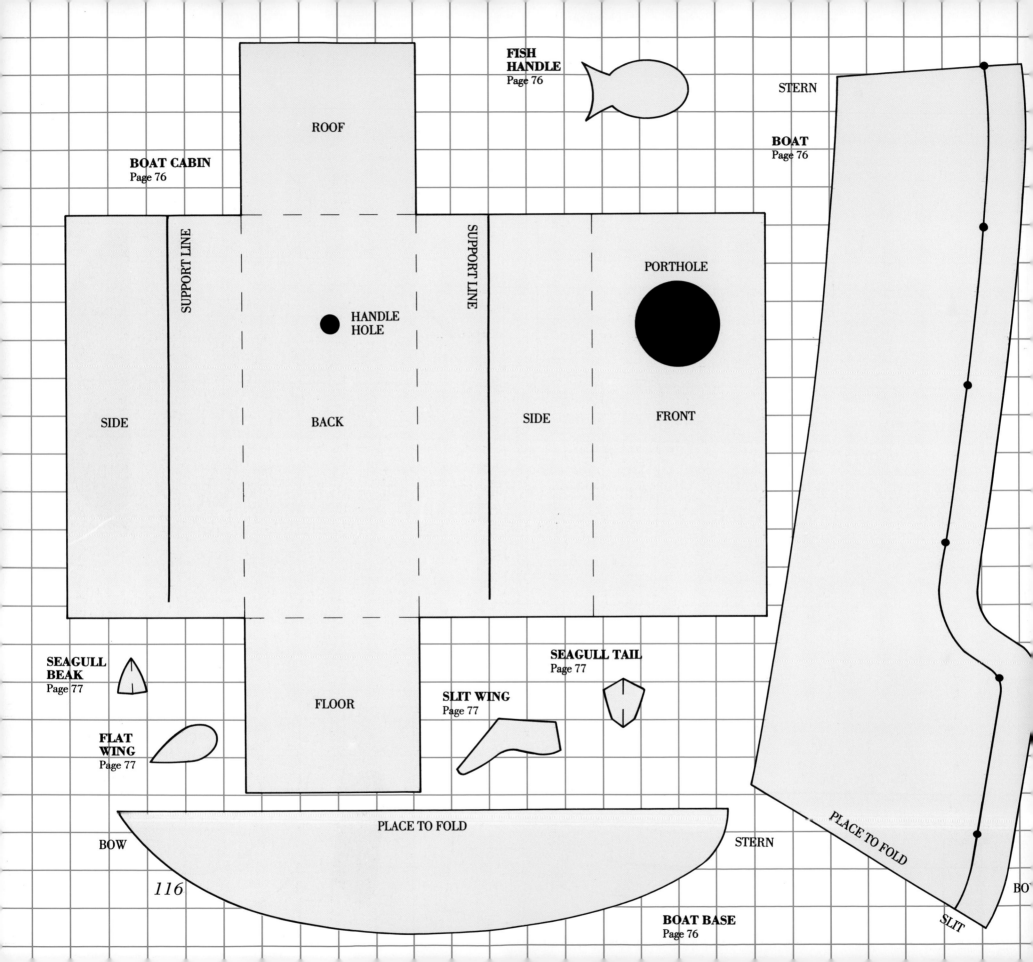

FISH HANDLE
Page 76

ROOF

BOAT CABIN
Page 76

SUPPORT LINE

SUPPORT LINE

HANDLE HOLE

PORTHOLE

SIDE

BACK

SIDE

FRONT

STERN

BOAT
Page 76

SEAGULL BEAK
Page 77

FLAT WING
Page 77

FLOOR

SLIT WING
Page 77

SEAGULL TAIL
Page 77

116

PLACE TO FOLD

BOW

STERN

BOAT BASE
Page 76

PLACE TO FOLD

SLIT

BO

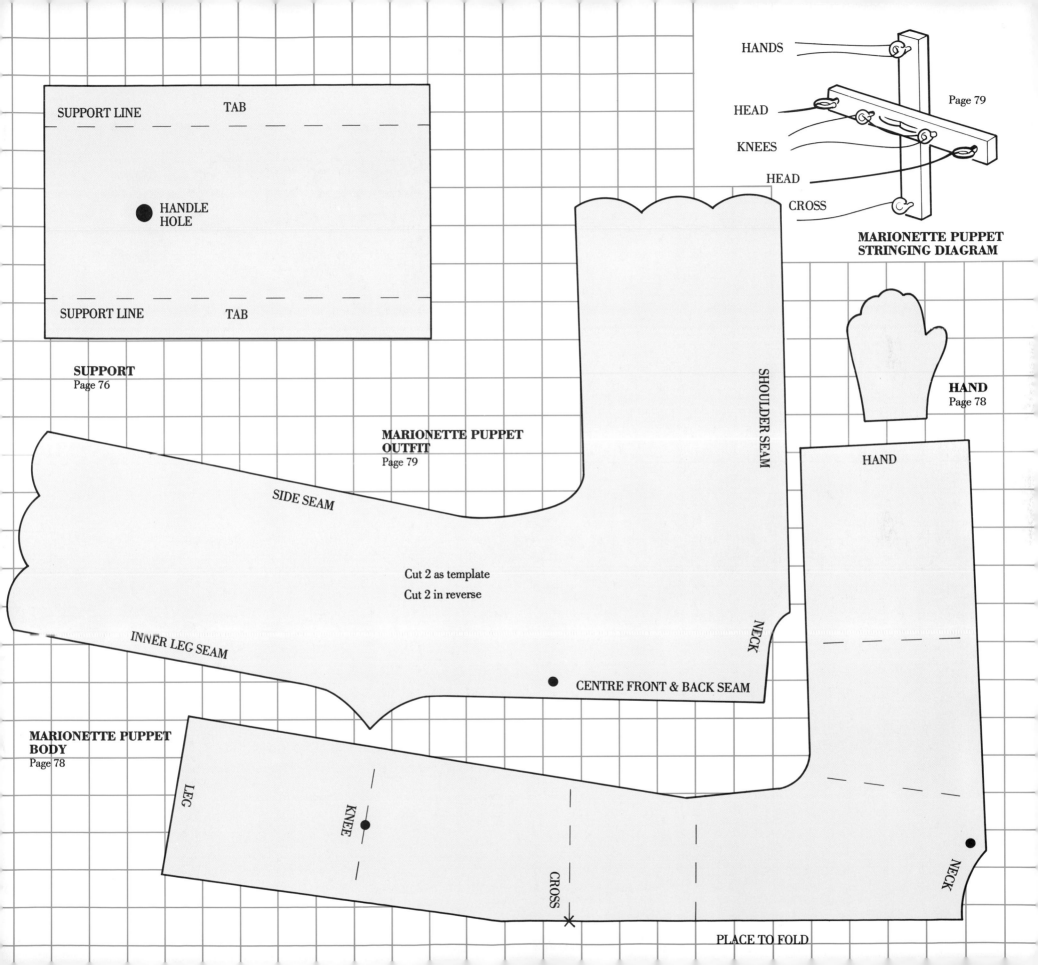

SUPPORT LINE   TAB

● HANDLE
    HOLE

SUPPORT LINE   TAB

SUPPORT
Page 76

HANDS

HEAD

KNEES

HEAD

CROSS

Page 79

**MARIONETTE PUPPET
STRINGING DIAGRAM**

HAND
Page 78

**MARIONETTE PUPPET
OUTFIT**
Page 79

SHOULDER SEAM

SIDE SEAM

HAND

Cut 2 as template

Cut 2 in reverse

NECK

INNER LEG SEAM

● CENTRE FRONT & BACK SEAM

**MARIONETTE PUPPET
BODY**
Page 78

LEG

KNEE

CROSS

NECK

✕

PLACE TO FOLD

STARFISH
Page 81

119

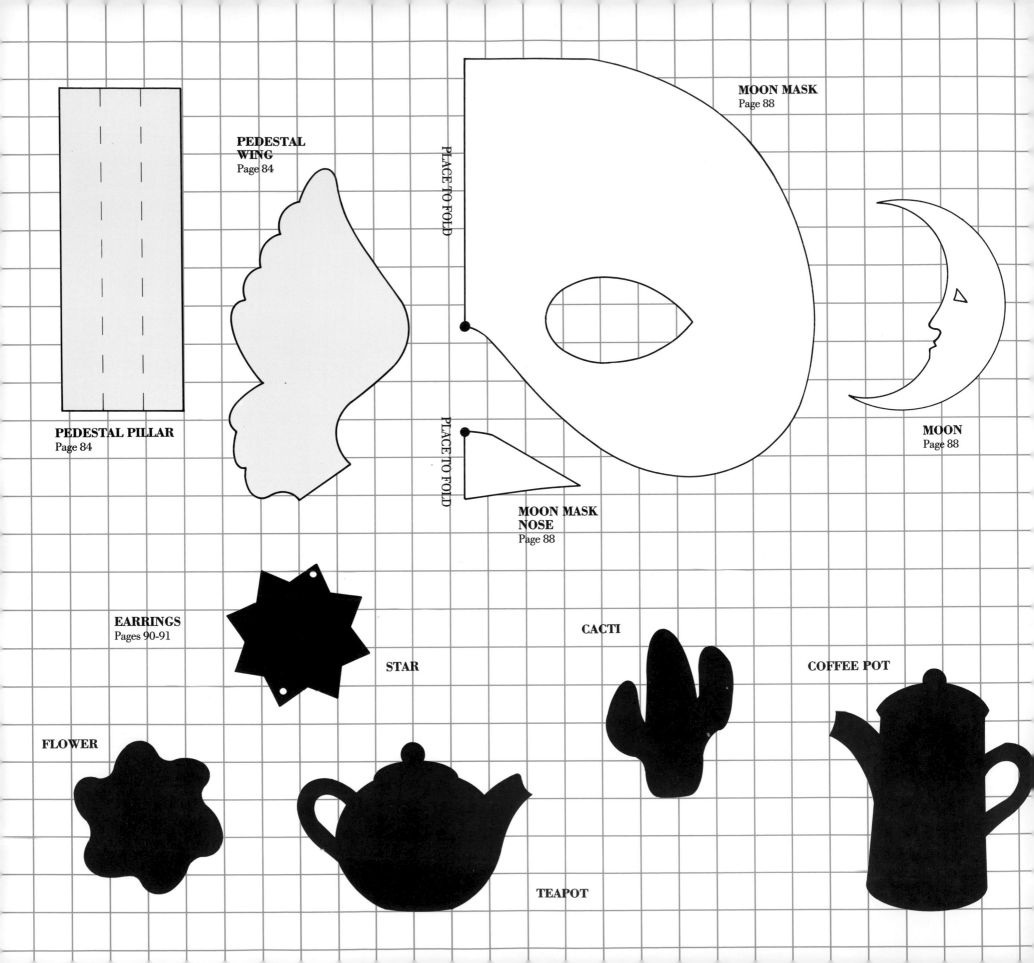

PEDESTAL WING
Page 84

PEDESTAL PILLAR
Page 84

PLACE TO FOLD

PLACE TO FOLD

MOON MASK
Page 88

MOON MASK NOSE
Page 88

MOON
Page 88

EARRINGS
Pages 90-91

STAR

CACTI

COFFEE POT

FLOWER

TEAPOT

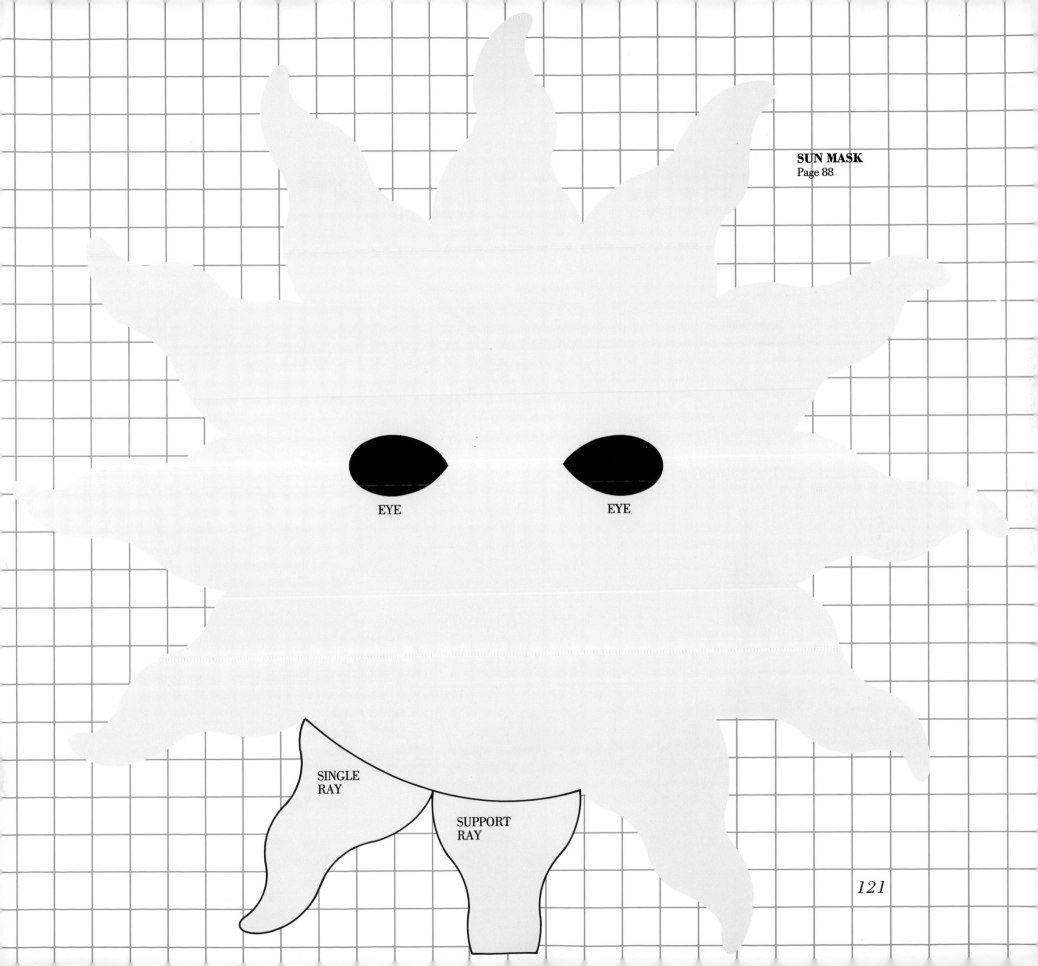

SUN MASK
Page 88

EYE

EYE

SINGLE RAY

SUPPORT RAY

121

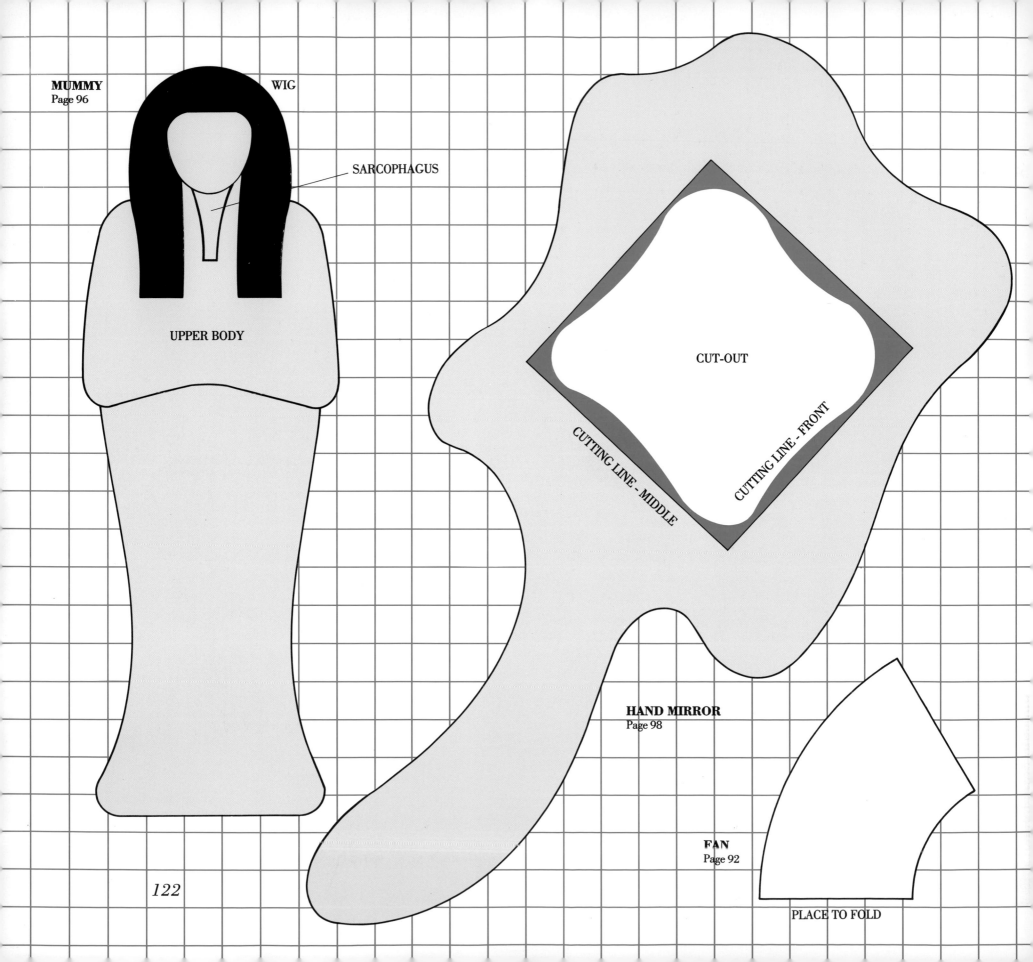

MUMMY
Page 96

WIG

SARCOPHAGUS

UPPER BODY

CUT-OUT

CUTTING LINE - MIDDLE

CUTTING LINE - FRONT

HAND MIRROR
Page 98

FAN
Page 92

PLACE TO FOLD

122

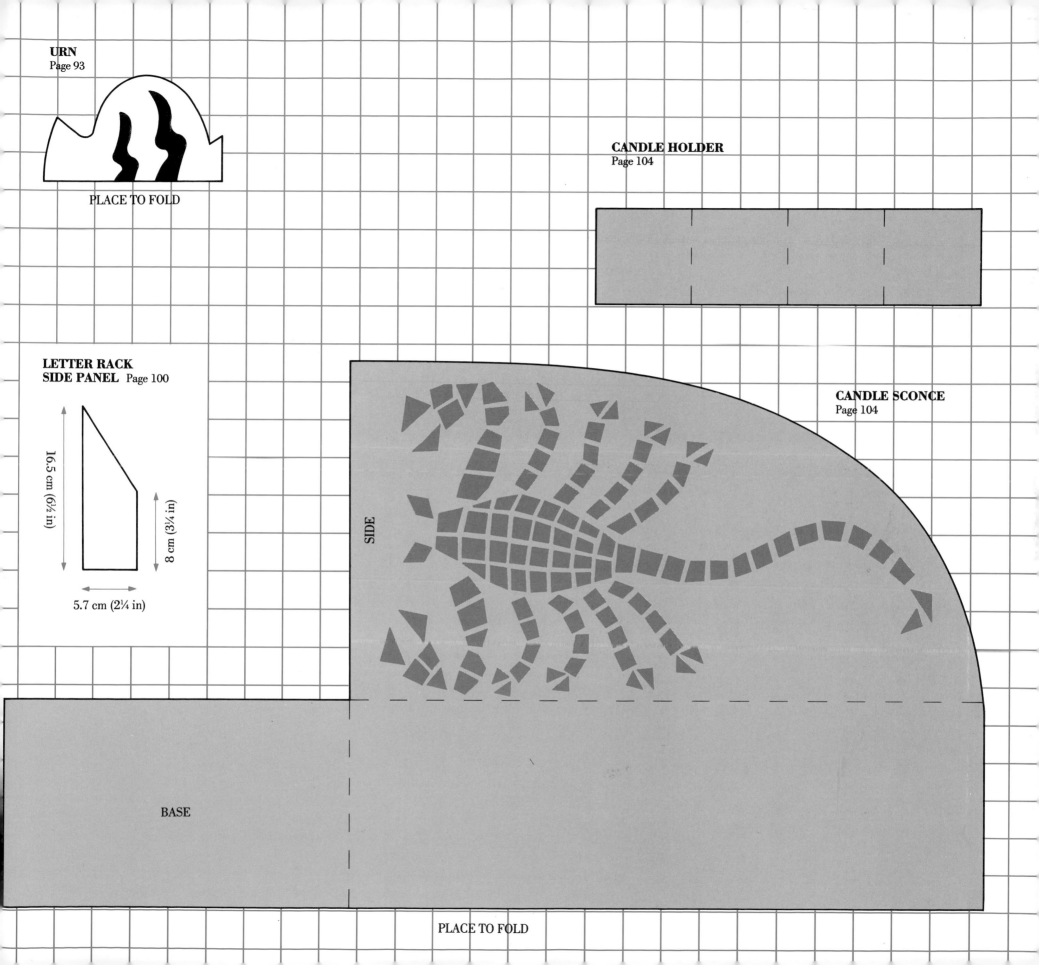

URN
Page 93

PLACE TO FOLD

CANDLE HOLDER
Page 104

**LETTER RACK
SIDE PANEL** Page 100

16.5 cm (6½ in)

8 cm (3¼ in)

5.7 cm (2¼ in)

CANDLE SCONCE
Page 104

SIDE

BASE

PLACE TO FOLD

Contributor: Phil Gorton

Managing Editor: Jo Finnis

Editor: Adèle Hayward

Design: Nigel Duffield

Photography: Steve Tanner

Photographic Direction: Nigel Duffield

Illustrations: Phil Gorton

Typesetting: Julie Smith

Production: Ruth Arthur; Sally Connolly;
Neil Randles; Jonathan Tickner

Director of Production: Gerald Hughes